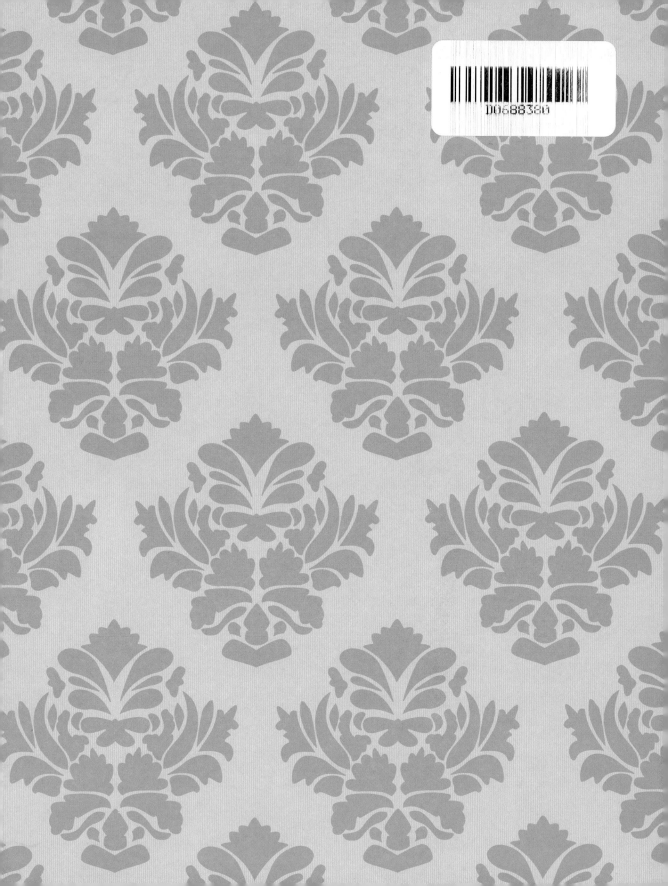

Deliciously Decorated

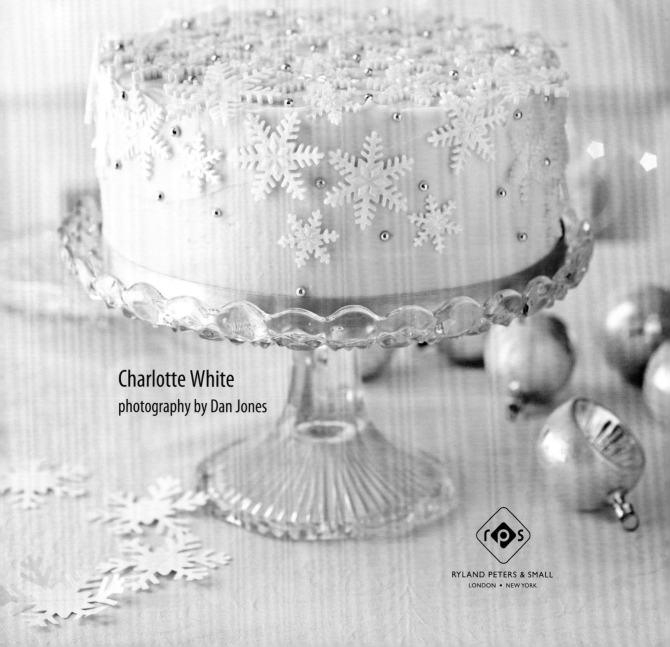

Deliciously Decorated

Over 40 delectable recipes for show-stopping
cakes, cupcakes and cookies

Charlotte White

photography by Dan Jones

RYLAND PETERS & SMALL
LONDON • NEW YORK

Designer Maria Lee-Warren
Commissioning Editor Nathan Joyce
Production Manager Gordana Simakovic
Art Director Leslie Harrington
Editorial Director Julia Charles
Publisher Cindy Richards

Prop Stylist Tony Hutchinson
Indexer Diana LeCore

First published in 2015
by Ryland Peters & Small
20–21 Jockey's Fields,
London WC1R 4BW
and
341 East 116th Street
New York, NY 10029
www.rylandpeters.com

10 9 8 7 6 5 4 3 2 1

ISBN: 978-1-84975-600-6

Printed and bound in China

A CIP record for this book is available from
the British Library.

US Library of Congress Cataloging-in-
Publication Data has been applied for.

Notes
• All spoon measurements are level, unless
otherwise specified.

• Ovens should be preheated to the specified
temperature. Recipes in this book were
tested using a regular oven. If using a
fan-assisted/convection oven, follow the
manufacturer's instructions for adjusting
temperatures.

• All eggs are medium (UK) or large (US),
unless otherwise specified. It is
recommended that free-range, organic eggs
be used whenever possible.

• All cake ingredients should be fresh and
used at room temperature. Take any
refrigerated ingredients, such as butter and
eggs out of the cold at least 1 hour before
you bake.

• The author uses particular brands of
Sugarflair and PME food colouring pastes, so
colour descriptions refer to these shades; if
you choose alternative brands, we suggest
that you use the photographs in this book to
match the colour.

• Most of the cake supplies used in this book
can be found through
www.globalsugarart.com, www.wilton.com,
www.cakedecoration.co.uk and
www.cakecraftworld.co.uk

Contents

Introduction

Keen bakers often tell me that they bake a delicious cake but 'oh, I can never make them as pretty as yours.' It is almost as if they mistakenly believe me to be in possession of magical powers or the keeper of some kind of mystical secret. Contrary to popular belief, I am no magician and I do not own an enchanted oven. What I do possess are a series of tricks that I use to transform my cakes into little works of edible art. In this book, I will share a series of techniques that will enable you to make your cakes look enchanting.

Cake decorating is, in essence, trickery — there is a piece of plastic that creates the perfect finish, a cutter to make this, a mould that makes that, special colours that make Red Velvet really really red, and so on. These are the tricks that a cake designer collects over years and I want to share them with you. As with any craft, practice will make perfect but, unlike in other crafts, you can simply devour any attempts that you are unhappy with!

I do not advocate the substitution of style for substance; your cake is intended to be eaten and should be delicious. My favourite recipes are included for you and I hope that these will become your go-to cakes for those occasions that require something exquisite.

Once you feel confident with these basic techniques, the potential for your cake design will be limitless. I have often said that I do not have an original idea in my head — all of my designs are inspired by the world around me. I look to art, fashion, history, design and the cinema to inform my choices of colour, motifs and even flavour. Once you start to see your jewellery box as a treasure trove of icing ideas, then you are ready to bake some truly magical cakes, cupcakes and cookies.

So leave your dark days of muggle cakes behind you, enrobe that naked cake, and let's make your cakes *Deliciously Decorated*.

Basic Recipes

Essential Equipment

A good cake designer is more akin to Batman than to Superman, because their superpowers lie mainly in the equipment that they have access to. You can create anything if you have the right piece of kit to craft it with. These few basic bits tucked into your utility belt will get you off to a flying start.

Cake drums: thick boards of 15-mm/$^5/_8$-in. thickness (generally baking foil-covered), which are available in any size to mount any cake upon.

Cake pans: the recipes in this book will all make sufficient batter for one cake baked in two standard 20-cm/8-in. round cake pans. As with all art, cake design is a slave to fashion and to achieve a deeper cake, increase all ingredient quantities by 50 per cent and bake in three 20-cm/8-in. cake pans. Baking times remain the same and all cake pans should be lined with parchment paper.

Chocolate cigarellos: sometimes difficult to find in supermarkets/grocery stores, but easy to buy online. They can always be substituted with chocolate finger biscuits for a quick and inexpensive treat. In either case, buy more than you need to allow for breakages in transit and nibbling in the kitchen.

Cookie cutters: I have used a 5-cm/2-in. round cookie cutter and a 5-cm/2-in. heart cookie cutter. If you use a smaller cutter, you will need to reduce your baking time. Larger cookies will require a longer baking time.

Cornflour/cornstarch: I use cornflour/cornstarch to prevent my sugarpaste from sticking to the work surface when rolling out. You can use icing/confectioners' sugar as an alternative, but this can be a little stickier in hot hands.

Dowelling rods: Foodsafe rods that can be inserted into lower cake tiers to carry the weight of higher tiers.

Freestanding mixer: if you already own one, you will know that these were heaven-sent to cream butter and sugar, or to mix royal icing to stiff peaks. If you don't own one, it's well worth the investment.

Glitters: keep a selection of edible glitters in your kit and use a matching colour glitter to your icing – contrasting colours sound great, but end up looking like grit! The exception is hologram white glitter, which goes with everything.

Lustres and dust colours: use these as dry dusts to brush detail onto sugar flowers and decorations, or mix with a little clear alcohol or water to create quick edible paints. I favour alcohol for this task as it evaporates far quicker than water, allowing me to build up my designs without a lengthy drying time.

Marzipan spacers: how do the professionals get a perfectly uniform thickness of icing on a cake? These wonderful plastic thickness guides are the answer. Never roll out without them!

Metallic food paint: use to paint metallic details on your designs.

Paste (or gel) colours: add colour to white sugarpaste or flower paste with a little paste colour on the end of a cocktail stick/toothpick. These highly concentrated colours have a long shelf life and are of professional quality. Never ever be tempted to use liquid colours or you will change the consistency of your sugarpaste and get rather sticky.

Piping bags: parchment piping bags are best for delicate royal icing work, while plastic ones are great for buttercream and chocolate ganache. In either case, disposable piping bags (see pages 38–39) are strongly recommended for the preservation of time and sanity.

Piping nozzles/tips: good quality metal piping nozzles/tips will last you a lifetime if cared for properly. Each project in this book lists the nozzle/tip that I have used to create the effect shown on the cake. Round, open star and leaf nozzles/tips are my favourites. With a small, medium and large version of each, you can create the most amazing designs.

Pizza wheel: the circular blade does not pull or drag the sugarpaste so this is the perfect tool for trimming excess and cutting straight lines.

Rolling pin: non-stick rolling pins made of food grade plastic are essential for working with sugarpaste, flower paste and modelling chocolate. These pins will not harbour any surprise moisture or texture the surface of your roll out like wooden ones can. You will need at least a 40-cm/16-in. rolling pin for covering cakes (50 cm/20 in. if you plan to work with larger cakes) and a smaller 15-cm/6-in. rolling pin for making smaller decorations.

Side scraper: a straight rectangular piece of metal or plastic, which is used to create perfectly straight edges in buttercream, frosting or ganache.

Straight-edged smoother: a small plastic 'iron' used to create a smooth finish on sugarpaste covered cakes.

Tilting turntable: another item that is truly heaven-sent for serial cake decorators. You will find intensive piping more comfortable using a turntable.

Tylose powder/CMC: knead 1 teaspoon into every 250 g/9 oz. sugarpaste to create a hard-drying modelling paste, perfect for small sugar flowers and moulded decorations. Your decorations will be hard enough to hold their shape but still soft enough to be pleasant to eat.

Sugar Flower Equipment

If you can master a selection of versatile sugar flowers, you will be able to create stunning cakes replete with decorations which can be kept as lifelong mementos; you may also be on the path to a long and happy career in cake design! There is a certain amount of equipment required to make flowers, but if well looked after, it will last you a lifetime.

Ball tool: your most trusty modelling tool, you will use this for frilling petals, adding movement and thinning the edge of your petals so they look authentically organic.

Blossom tint dust colours: colour in dry dust form is great for adding depth to your flowers.

Cel stick/pin: thicker than a cocktail stick/toothpick but thinner than a small rolling pin, this is used for rolling out tiny petals and adding minute details.

Cocktail sticks/toothpicks: infinitely useful for a number of tasks.

Cutters: you will need a selection of petal and leaf cutters to make flowers and I have listed the ones that have been used for each project. Look after your cutters by cleaning them frequently in hot, soapy water and drying them thoroughly before storing. Good-quality plastic or metal cutters should last you a lifetime so think of these as investment pieces.

Edible glue: can be bought in small pots or made by mixing 1 part CMC tylose powder to 30 parts boiling water. Mix thoroughly and leave for 12 hours before using.

Floristry tape: green and brown are the most useful colours to have in your kit. Used for binding stems of flowers together, floristry tape is not glued and only sticks to itself when pulled tightly. To tape a wire, gently pinch the end of your tape at the top of your wire and pull the tape taut with your other hand — slowly spinning the wire, while keeping the tape taut, will bind the wire.

Foam mat: used for adding detail to petals, where a soft surface is required.

Non-stick board: used for rolling out flower paste.

Paintbrushes: in a variety of sizes and widths for everything from applying edible glue to tinting with dust colours.

Polystyrene cel buds and balls: used as the central part of large flowers such as roses and peonies, these reduce the amount of flower paste that you need and result in a lighter flower. I have listed the correct size to use for each project.

Round nose pliers: for bending thin wires. You can get away with using clean tweezers for this, but these are more comfortable.

Small non-stick rolling pin: 15 cm/6 in. is quite large enough.

Small wire cutters: a very useful tool, but a pair of scissors will also do nicely, provided that you don't mind blunting them!

Vegetable shortening and cornflour/cornstarch: you may find that you need something to prevent your flower/gum paste from sticking BUT exercise caution here as too much of either of these will ruin your paste (and it is pricey stuff!), and use the tiniest amount of shortening or cornflour/cornstarch on your non-stick board or the tiniest dab of cornflour on hot hands if required.

Wires: you will need to select the appropriate gauge (thickness) for the size of flower that you are making. As a general rule, use a heavy wire such as #20 gauge for large flowers and a lighter #30 gauge for smaller blossoms. I have mentioned the best gauges to use for each project.

FLOWER PASTE AND MODELLING PASTE

It is important to use the correct type of paste for the flower that you are making. With each project, I have listed the correct paste to use but here is a little explanation as to the properties of each one.

Flower/gum paste: This is the best paste to use for making delicate wired flowers that you have no intention of eating. Despite being made from sugar, flower paste (also known as floristry paste) is decidedly unappetizing and dries hard enough to break teeth!

Because flower paste dries as hard as porcelain, decorations made from this can be kept for a lifetime, providing they are stored safely and out of sunlight, which causes colour fading. The disadvantage of working with flower paste is that it can dry out very quickly, becoming unusable, which means that you have to be very diligent in storing any paste that you are not working with in an airtight bag, and working fairly quickly.

Modelling paste 50/50: One way to avoid the problem of flower paste drying out is to combine it with an equal amount of sugarpaste and knead together to form a modelling paste. This paste will dry more securely than sugarpaste would, meaning that you can roll it thinner and make more intricate flowers with this, but will stay a little softer whilst working. This paste is fine for making smaller pulled flowers and simple blossoms but will not be suitable for making larger wired flowers.

Sugarpaste with CMC powder: By kneading a teaspoon of CMC powder into 250 g/9 oz. of sugarpaste, you will create a versatile paste for modelling. Sugarpaste decorations made using this extra addition will dry hard and retain their shape. This kind of paste is perfect for producing shapes from silicone moulds that are intended for eating as this is by far the tastiest option for modelling!

Classic Victoria Sponge Cake

340 g/3 sticks unsalted butter
340 g/1¾ cups
    caster/granulated sugar
6 large eggs
2 teaspoons vanilla extract
340 g/2⅔ cups self-
    raising/rising flour
1½ teaspoons baking powder
6 tablespoons whole milk

2 x 20-cm/8-in. round cake pans

*Makes 1 x 20-cm/
8-in. cake**

There are few things in life that are more disappointing that a dry slice of Victoria Sponge Cake. That's why I won't make one! This recipe is foolproof and the result is fluffy, light and moist. Whip up this cake for an afternoon teatime treat that is sure to delight your guests.

1 Preheat the oven to 180°C (350°F) Gas 4.

2 Cream the butter and sugar together until they are pale and creamy. Never underestimate the time that it will take to complete this step. Allow 5 minutes using a freestanding mixer with a paddle attachment or 5–7 minutes using an electric handwhisk. If you want to opt for manual power, beat vigorously with a wooden spoon until cream-like and your arm falls off.

3 Add one egg at a time, allowing each egg to be fully incorporated before adding the next. This patience should prevent curdling.

4 Stir the vanilla extract into your mixture.

5 Sift the flour and baking powder into a separate bowl and fold into your wet ingredients by hand. Be gentle and stop mixing as soon as the flour is incorporated.

6 Add a little milk to make a dropping consistency – the cake mixture should dollop off of your wooden spoon like thick cream. Divide this mixture between 2 round cake pans and bake for 35–40 minutes or until the cakes are risen and a cocktail stick/toothpick inserted into the cake comes out clean. Allow the cakes to cool in their pans for 5 minutes before turning out onto a wire rack. A 15-cm/6-in. cake will need 25–30 minutes and cupcakes will take approximately 20 minutes to bake.

* Halve all quantities for a 15-cm/6-in. cake or 12 cupcakes

Lemon Drizzle Cake

300 g/2½ sticks unsalted butter, at room temperature

400 g/2 cups caster/granulated sugar

8 large eggs

zest and freshly squeezed juice of 3 lemons

8 tablespoons lemon curd

300 g/2⅓ cups self-raising/rising flour

250 g/2 cups ground almonds

2 teaspoons baking powder

For the lemon syrup:
freshly squeezed juice of 4 lemons

120 g/⅔ cup caster/granulated sugar

2 x 20-cm/8-in. round cake pans lined with baking parchment

Makes 1 x 20-cm/ 8-in. cake*

I absolutely adore Lemon Drizzle Cake. This one somehow manages to be light and zesty, positively bursting with lemon, while also being sweet and slightly sticky. Doesn't that sound like everything a lemon cake should be?

1 Preheat the oven to 160°C (325°F) Gas 3.

2 Cream the butter and sugar together until almost white. Seriously, the minute you think you are done creaming, add on another 3 minutes! This is best done in a free-standing mixer or, at the very least, with an electric handwhisk.

3 Beat the eggs in a jug/pitcher and add the lemon zest and juice to this. Gradually incorporate this liquid into the butter and sugar, mixing continuously on a low speed. If the mixture starts to curdle, add a tablespoon of your flour to bring it back together.

4 Add the lemon curd and mix through.

5 Combine your dry ingredients in a separate bowl and fold these into the wet mixture a third at a time.

6 Divide the mixture between the cake pans and bake for approximately 45 minutes (a 15-cm/6-in. cake will take 35–40 minutes). The cakes are done when a skewer comes out clean.

7 To make the lemon syrup, heat the lemon juice and sugar in a saucepan over a low heat, stirring occasionally, until the sugar has completely dissolved and the syrup is perfectly translucent.

8 As soon as you remove the cakes from the oven, poke them right down to the bottom of the pan in several places with a skewer. Really go for it and pour all of the syrup over the top of the cakes but leave each pouring of syrup to soak in before you add more rather than allowing a puddle to collect on top. Leave the cakes to cool in their pans for 10 minutes before turning out onto a wire rack to cool completely.

* Halve all quantities for a 15-cm/6-in. cake or 12 cupcakes

Red Velvet Cake

1 tablespoon cider vinegar

720 ml/3 cups soya/soy milk

600 g/4⅔ cups plain/
    all-purpose flour

600 g/2 cups
    caster/granulated sugar

50 g/⅓ cup plus 1
    tablespoon cocoa powder

1½ teaspoons baking powder

1½ teaspoons bicarbonate
    of/baking soda

1½ teaspoons salt

240 ml/1 cup sunflower oil

2 teaspoons Red Extra food
    colour paste diluted in
    6 tablespoons boiling water

2 tablespoons vanilla extract

1 teaspoon almond extract

*2 x 20-cm/8-in. round cake
pans lined with baking
parchment*

*Makes 1 x 20-cm/
8-in. cake**

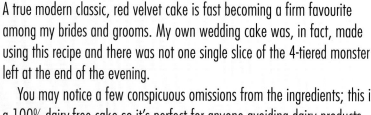

A true modern classic, red velvet cake is fast becoming a firm favourite among my brides and grooms. My own wedding cake was, in fact, made using this recipe and there was not one single slice of the 4-tiered monster left at the end of the evening.

　　You may notice a few conspicuous omissions from the ingredients; this is a 100% dairy-free cake so it's perfect for anyone avoiding dairy products from their diet. Please do not think that this cake will be at all lacking in flavour.... ah, I cannot convince you with my words except to say that you will really love this cake when you taste it. Even the most hardened sceptic has fallen victim to its charms!

1 Preheat the oven to 180°C (350°F) Gas 4.

2 Whisk the cider vinegar into the soya/soy milk and set aside to curdle a little while you prepare the dry ingredients.

3 Measure the flour, sugar, cocoa, baking powder and bicarbonate of/baking soda and salt into a bowl and stir to combine, making a small well in the centre.

4 Spoon the red food colouring paste** into a small bowl (preferably a glass bowl that can be thrown straight into the dishwasher afterwards) and add the boiling water, stirring calmly to encourage the colour to dilute. Leave this aside to cool slightly.

5 Add the sunflower oil, vanilla extract and almond essence to the curdled soy milk. Stir the diluted red food colouring into the wet ingredients.

6 Pour all of the wet ingredients into the well that you have made in the dry ingredients. Stir decisively with a wooden spoon until all of the dry ingredients are incorporated. By now, your kitchen should look like a scene from Sweeney Todd. Avoid answering the door; you may look terrifying.

7 Divide the mixture between 2 round cake pans and bake in the preheated oven for 35 minutes (a 15-cm/6-in. cake will need 25–30 minutes and cupcakes will take 15–20 minutes to bake) or until a skewer comes out clean. Allow the cakes to cool in their pans for 5 minutes before turning out onto a wire rack.

* Halve all quantities for a 15-cm/6-in. cake or 12 cupcakes

** Red Extra paste will give you a far stronger red hue than supermarket liquid food colouring, which often results in a brownish cake.

Chocolate Mud Cake

220 g/7½ oz. dark/bittersweet chocolate

220 g/1 stick plus 6 tablespoons unsalted butter

2 tablespoons instant coffee granules

160 ml/⅔ cup water

125 g/1 cup plain/all-purpose flour

125 g/1 cup self-raising/rising flour

40 g/⅓ cup cocoa powder

½ teaspoon bicarbonate of/baking soda

480 g/2⅓ cups caster/granulated sugar

pinch of salt

4 large eggs

2 tablespoons plus 1 teaspoon vegetable oil

110 ml/scant ½ cup buttermilk

2 x 20-cm/8-in. round cake pans lined with baking parchment

Makes 1 x 20-cm/ 8-in. cake*

The feedback that I've received since first sharing this recipe in my first book has been so amazing that I could not bear to leave it out of this one! This recipe may appear complex at first glance but please trust me and know that it is straightforward, delicious, and waiting to become your new favourite. Oh, and you will thank me when your kitchen is filled with the most divine scent of chocolate cake!

1 Preheat the oven to 160°C (325°F) Gas 3.

2 Melt the chocolate and the butter in a small saucepan with the instant coffee granules and 160 ml/⅔ cup water. Keep the temperature low and turn off the heat when only a few small lumps remain – these will melt in the heat of the mixture and turning the heat off early prevents burning.

3 Measure the flours, cocoa, bicarbonate of/baking soda and sugar into a bowl with the salt. Make a small well in the centre and set aside.

4 Beat the eggs, oil and buttermilk together in a jug/pitcher before tipping this mixture into the dry ingredients and stirring it into a thick paste.

5 Pour the melted chocolate and butter mixture on top of this paste and bring everything together with a wooden spoon until you have one glossy mixture in the bowl.

6 Pour the batter into the 2 prepared cake pans. Bake in the preheated oven for 45–50 minutes or until a skewer comes out clean (or with only a few tiny crumbs attached to it). A 15-cm/6-in. cake will take approximately 35–40 minutes to bake. Allow the cake to cool completely in its pans.

* Halve all quantities for a 15-cm/6-in. cake or 12 cupcakes

Salted Caramel Cake

For the caramel syrup:
225 g/1 stick plus 2
   tablespoons
   caster/granulated sugar
250 ml/1 cup boiling water

For the caramel cake:
225 g/1 stick plus 6
   tablespoons unsalted butter
380 g/2 cups less
   2 tablespoons
   caster/granulated sugar
4 UK large/US extra large
   eggs
480 g/3¾ cups plain/all-
   purpose flour
1 tablespoon baking powder
½ teaspoon salt
250 ml/1 cup whole milk
2 teaspoons caramel essence
   or 1 teaspoon vanilla
   extract

*2 x 20-cm/8-in. round cake
pans lined with baking
parchment*

*Makes 1 x 20 cm/
8 in. cake**

Be careful while caramelizing that sugar, kids! It is so worth it for this delicious cake in which the flavour of caramel runs right through the cake itself, as well as in the frosting.

1 Preheat the oven to 180°C (350°F) Gas 4.

2 First make the caramel syrup. Use a heavy-bottomed saucepan to heat your sugar until it goes brown and treacly, a little darker than golden/light corn syrup, with no lumps. Stir every now and then but do not leave the room while the sugar is heating as it will go from nicely caramelized to burnt and ruined very quickly!

3 Add the boiling water very carefully as the pan will spit. Try pouring the water down the side of the saucepan and wear an oven glove if you are nervous or clumsy (I am often both!).

4 Stir the water into the syrup for around 1 minute until the two have completely combined. Remove the pan from the heat and allow the syrup to cool. You can make the syrup 1–2 days in advance if you like and store in an airtight container until needed.

5 To make the cake, first cream the butter and the sugar until you have a pale and creamy mixture. This process should take around 5 minutes in a freestanding mixer or using an electric whisk and allowing a little time to mix thoroughly will set you up for a wonderfully light cake.

6 Add the eggs, one at a time, making sure that each one is fully incorporated before adding the next.

7 Add 125 ml/½ cup of your caramel syrup to the mixture and beat briefly until smooth and golden. You will need the remaining syrup for your Salted Caramel Buttercream (see page 20).

8 Sift your flour, baking powder and salt into another bowl and measure your milk and caramel essence into a jug/pitcher. Fold in one-third of your dry ingredients into the cake mixture followed by one half of your milk and essence. Add another third of your dry ingredients, followed by the remaining milk. Remember to stir well after each addition to ensure that all ingredients are incorporated. Finish off with the final third of your dry ingredients.

9 Divide your cake mixture between 2 round cake pans and bake for 35–45 minutes (a 15-cm/6-in. cake will need 25–30 minutes). The cake is done when it has risen beautifully and a skewer comes out clean.

10 Cool the cakes in their pans for 5 minutes before turning out onto a wire rack.

* Halve all quantities for a 15-cm/6-in. cake or 12 cupcakes

Basic Cookies

200 g/1 stick plus 6
   tablespoons unsalted butter
200 g/1 cup golden
   caster/raw cane sugar
1 egg
optional flavourings: 1 vanilla
   pod, 50 g/⅓ cup cocoa
   powder or grated zest of
   1 lemon
400 g/3 cups plus 2
   tablespoons plain/all-
   purpose flour – reduce this
   amount by 50 g/⅓ cup if
   making chocolate cookies

marzipan spacers
non-stick rolling pin
5-cm/2-in. cookie cutter
baking sheet lined with baking
   parchment

Makes 12 cookies

Keep it simple, stupid! These cookies are basic and versatile and they come out perfectly every time. Just remember to allow the dough enough time to chill in the fridge before you use it.

1 Preheat the oven to 180°C (350°F) Gas 4.

2 Begin by creaming the butter and sugar in a freestanding mixer or with an electric whisk. Allow for 3 minutes of beating to ensure that the two are fully combined. I use golden caster/raw cane sugar because I think that this creates a deeper flavour but you can use regular caster/granulated sugar if you prefer. You can do this by hand but be prepared for a workout.

3 Add the egg and beat until incorporated.

4 At this point, you can add your desired flavouring: vanilla, chocolate or lemon

5 Add the flour and beat until the mixture forms a ball of dough. Remove the dough from your mixer and wrap tightly in clingfilm/plastic wrap. This will need to chill in the fridge for at least 30 minutes before you use it. You can make your dough up to 1 week in advance.

6 Roll out your dough on a floured surface, using marzipan spacers to give you an even thickness. Do not be tempted to knead your dough to warm it up – you will need to work hard to flatten this cold dough but it needs to be cold for the cookies to hold their shape.

7 Cut out 12 cookies using the cookie cutter and lay these on the prepared baking sheet. If you have time, put this sheet into the fridge for 10 minutes before you bake.

8 These cookies will take around 10 minutes to bake and are ready when they are golden brown and firm. Allow the cookies to cool completely on a wire rack before storing in an airtight container. You can store these cookies for up to 2 weeks, if you can resist them!

Basic Buttercream

250 g/2 sticks unsalted butter

250–350 g/2–3 cups icing/confectioners' sugar

optional flavourings:

Vanilla Buttercream
2 teaspoons good-quality vanilla extract or the seeds from 1 vanilla pod

Chocolate Buttercream
50 g/$\frac{1}{3}$ cup unsweetened cocoa powder

Lemon Buttercream
2 tablespoons lemon curd

Salted Caramel Buttercream
125 ml/$\frac{1}{2}$ cup caramel syrup (see page 18)

$\frac{1}{2}$ teaspoon fine table salt

Makes enough for 1 x 20-cm/8-in. cake or 24 cupcakes

All buttercreams begin in the same way. I have added a few basic flavour alterations to allow you use your buttercream to complement your cake. I like to beat my buttercream for a good 5 minutes to really fuse the icing/confectioners' sugar and butter together so that the end result is light, smooth and deliciously creamy.

1 Roughly carve up the butter and beat in a freestanding mixer for 3 minutes until creamy. You can also do this using a handheld electric mixer or by hand, although you'll find that the latter takes much longer.

2 At this point, you can add your desired flavouring: vanilla, chocolate, lemon or caramel.

3 Once your flavour is fully incorporated, add 250 g/2 generous cups icing/confectioners' sugar and beat for 1 minute. Check the consistency of your buttercream — you are aiming for the thickness of thick whipped cream — if your buttercream is too runny, add another 100 g/1 cup icing/confectioners' sugar. You will then need to beat the buttercream for a further 5 minutes, until the icing/confectioners' sugar is completely incorporated.

Cream Cheese Frosting

250 g/2 sticks unsalted butter

250 g/9 oz. full-fat cream cheese

750 g/6¼ cups icing/confectioners' sugar

Makes enough for 1 x 20-cm/8-in. cake or 24 cupcakes

This is the only way to complement Red Velvet cake. However, I promise that if you try this in place of basic buttercream in your Victoria Sponge Cake, you will never go back!

1 Roughly carve up the butter and beat in a freestanding mixer for 3 minutes until creamy. You can also do this using a handheld electric mixer or by hand, although you'll find that the latter takes much longer.

2 Add 250 g/2 generous cups of icing/confectioners' sugar and beat until fully combined.

3 Spoon the cream cheese (yes, you need to use full fat, this is not a diet option!) into the buttercream mixture and beat until combined. You may find that the mixture goes wet and soupy, or that it starts to look like it is curdling – please do not worry in either case.

4 Add another 250 g/2 generous cups of icing/confectioners' sugar and beat until fully combined, scraping down the sides at least once.

5 Remove your beaters from the frosting and test by running a finger through the mixture; your finger should leave a trail that holds in the frosting. You are aiming for a thick whipped cream consistency so add more icing/confectioners' sugar if the mixture is too runny.

6 Once you are happy with the consistency of your frosting, I recommend that you allow another 2 minutes of beating to create a beautifully smooth consistency.

Chocolate Ganache

500 g/16 oz. dark/bittersweet chocolate (minimum of 70% cocoa solids) OR 750 g/ 24 oz. white chocolate (good quality, the cheap stuff misbehaves!)

250 ml/1 cup whipping cream

Makes enough for 1 x 20-cm/8-in. cake or 12 cupcakes*

A delicious and rich alternative to buttercream, ganache is perfect for the chocoholic in your life! Start with a dark chocolate ganache and progress to white chocolate as you will find that the higher cocoa content acts as a stabilizer making this the more reliable option.

1 Finely chop the chocolate and set aside.

2 Heat the cream to just short of boiling point in a clean bowl set over a saucepan of simmering water. The water in your saucepan should be only 2.5-cm/1-in. deep and not touch the bottom of your bowl. You can also do this cautiously in a microwave.

3 Remove the bowl from the heat and add the chocolate to the cream. Wait for a minute to allow the heat to begin melting the chocolate before slowly stirring until all of the chocolate is incorporated into a glossy mixture. If any stubborn lumps remain, return the ganache to the heat and the saucepan for 1–2 minutes, stirring and watching closely.

4 Allow to cool for 5 minutes, or until the consistency of your ganache is similar to buttercream.

* Halve all quantities for a 15-cm/6-in. cake

Marshmallow Meringue Frosting

4 large egg whites

120 ml/$\frac{1}{2}$ cup golden/light corn syrup

250 g/1$\frac{1}{4}$ cups caster/granulated sugar

$\frac{1}{2}$ teaspoon salt

$\frac{1}{2}$ teaspoon cream of tartar

2 teaspoon vanilla extract

Makes enough for 1 x 20-cm/8-in. cake or 1 x 6-in. two-tiered cake*

When rustic looking buttercreamed wedding cakes came into vogue, I knew that I was going to need to find a way to approach this with a little bit of a difference. Cue my Marshmallow Meringue Frosting. This sticky, sweet and dangerously moreish frosting began life as Nigella's suggested topping for a cupcake in her book *Feast*. I loved making this topping and had not thought about it in years – until the aforementioned conundrum occurred. What if I made this frosting and slathered it on a wedding cake? The result was a hit; a sticky, slick and gooey hit that can only be eaten with a fork, but a hit nonetheless. This frosting does not set but remains soft and sticky, without losing its shape. Frankly, it has to be tried to be believed.

1 Put all of the ingredients, with the exception of the vanilla, into a large glass mixing bowl.

2 Prepare a large saucepan with 7.5 cm/3 in. of simmering water and set the bowl over the top.

3 Whisk the mixture with a handheld mixer on high speed over the heat of the simmering water until the frosting holds stiff little peaks. This will take around 10 minutes and you will think that I have gone insane – please trust me that the pale yellow slop in your bowl will transform into a wonderfully white glossy meringue.

4 Once you are happy that the frosting is holding peaks, remove the bowl from the heat and whisk in your vanilla (the very best quality that you can afford) for 1–2 minutes as the frosting cools. By this point your bowl should be filled with the most gloriously thick and shiny frosting with an intoxicating aroma of vanilla. This can then be spread thickly over cakes or dolloped generously on cupcakes. Whichever you choose, I bet you cannot resist licking the bowl.

* Halve all quantities for a 15-cm/6-in. cake

Basic Techniques

Levelling, Filling & Crumb-coating a Cake

You may have noticed that the cakes on these pages do not look much like the cakes that first come out of your oven. There is no sorcery involved here and I do not own an enchanted oven that turns out perfectly level cakes upon every baking. What I do possess are a few helpful techniques for removing unsightly peaks and creating a solid foundation for icing. In much the same way as good underwear eradicates bumps and bulging in your final outfit, so too will the time invested in preparing your cake for icing result in a far smoother finish.

20-cm/8-in. or 15-cm/6-in. cake, baked in 2 layers

1 quantity Basic Buttercream (see page 20)

jam (if you fancy it)

15-cm/8-in. or 20-cm/6-in. cake drum/circle (to match the diameter of your cake)
icing turntable (optional)
large (sharp) serrated knife
large palette knife
side scraper

1 Ensure that your cakes have cooled completely before you begin and that you have removed any baking parchment. Place the first cake onto a cake drum/circle secured with a small dab of buttercream, and mount on an icing turntable (if you have one). The cake drum/circle should be of the same diameter as the cake itself.

2 You should find that your cake has risen to a peak in its centre. If you follow the peak down to the edges of your cake, you should be able to find the point at which the cake started to rise. Lay your serrated knife horizontally at this point and press very gently into the cake.

3 With one hand on your knife and the other laid flat on the top of your cake, hold your knife still but slowly rotate the cake to create a guideline all around the edge. You want to apply just enough pressure to leave an indentation.

4 Continue rotating your cake and allow your knife to press into the cake a little more each time you make a full turn. By cutting in towards the centre of the cake at all times and holding your knife still, you should get a perfectly level cake without damaging any of the edges. (**A**)

5 Repeat steps 1–4 with your other cake. You may find it useful to use your already levelled cake as a height guide for making your first cut to ensure that your 2 cake layers are the same height.

6 Spread a thin coating of buttercream on the cut side of one of your cakes. It is a very common mistake to be over-generous at this point — if you fill your cake with too much buttercream, when it is covered with icing it will develop a bulge around the middle. This is a result of the buttercream 'relaxing' and moving in-between the layers of your cake. I promise that you will only need a thin spreading. (**B**)

A

B

7 If you are using jam, spread a thin coating on the cut side of your second cake layer. Ideally, this should be thin enough that you can still see the cake beneath it.

8 Sandwich your cake layers together (with all fillings in the middle). Ensure that your cake is perfectly aligned and level at the top. If this is a lower tier of a larger cake, it's a good idea to use a spirit level to check the cake is even. It may sound pedantic but it will ensure success!

9 Now for the fun bit, known as crumb-coating as it keeps any crumbs safely within. Dollop a good helping of buttercream on the top of your cake, which you'll use almost as a reservoir of buttercream. (**C**)

C

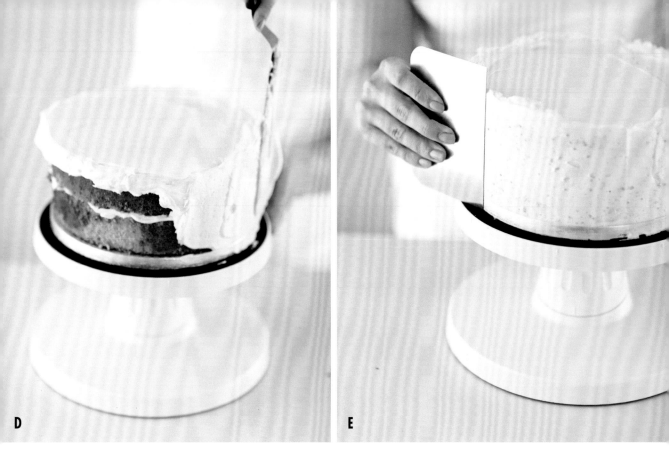

D

E

10 Take a generous amount of this buttercream from the top of the cake with a large palette knife and slather it around the sides of your cake, being careful to fill the small gap around the bottom edge of your cake. Spread a very thick layer of buttercream around the whole cake and over the top; use more than you need as the next stage is an exercise in taking away the excess. (**D**)

11 Using a side scraper tool with its long edge pressed against the drum/circle beneath your cake and its short edge stood flush against the work surface, pull the scraper towards you around the cake and remove the excess buttercream (**E**). Always scrape towards you so that it is apparent when the scraper needs to be cleaned off – you cannot hope to remove buttercream from your cake with a dirty scraper. Wipe the excess buttercream from your scraper as often as you need to and continue around the cake until you have perfectly straight sides in line with the drum beneath your cake, which should now appear to be part of the cake itself.

12 Scrape the top edges in towards the centre of your cake in short strokes. Wipe your scraper after each stroke and be careful to check that you are creating a level top. Once you are happy with your crumb-coated cake, refrigerate for 1 hour to set firm before moving on. (**F**)

13 If you want to create a buttercreamed cake with a more rustic appearance, press the tip of your palette knife against the sides of your cake and rotate the turntable (or the cake drum/circle if you haven't got one). Start at the top edge of your cake and move down the sides gradually with each rotation. (**G**)

F

G

Frosted Cakes

Frosted cakes covered with buttercream, ganache, cream cheese or marshmallow meringue frostings are a popular choice for those who are not keen on the taste of sugarpaste icing or who want a slightly less formal look.

Sugarpaste does have the advantage of creating a protective layer preventing your cake from drying out, but buttercream, ganache, cream cheese or marshmallow meringue frosted cakes do not have the same advantage. As such, frosted cakes will not keep for the same length of time as sugarpaste cakes will. If you are able to, I recommend baking your cake the day before you intend to serve it and decorating it on the morning

of delivery for optimum freshness. Remember that you can make all of your decorations, such as sugar flowers, in advance, so this early start need not be a mad panic!

Frosted cakes do not need to be stored in the fridge — just keep them somewhere cool and dry — unless you live with particularly high temperatures and humidity. If the temperature is unusually high, it is sometimes necessary to refrigerate the decorated cake for a short time. Remember to take your cake out of the fridge at least 30 minutes before you plan to serve to allow it to come back to room temperature.

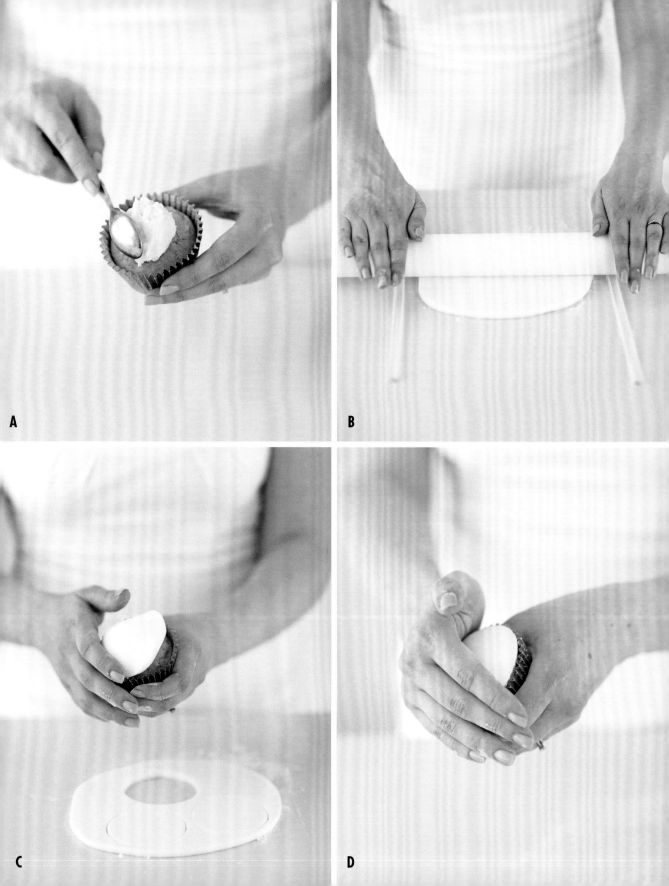

A

B

C

D

Covering a Cupcake in Sugarpaste

I tend to refer to my cupcakes as 'Fondant Fancy Cupcakes' because they remind me a little of these classic British treats. When decorating a cupcake, the sugarpaste covering provides a clean and modern top, hiding a secret surprise of buttercream beneath, which is just sufficient to delight without setting the teeth on edge.

500 g/1 lb. sugarpaste (per dozen cupcakes)

½ quantity of Buttercream or Cream Cheese Frosting (see pages 20–21)

cornflour/cornstarch, for dusting

small palette knife
large non-stick rolling pin
marzipan spacers (see page 32)
5-cm/2-in. round cookie cutter

1 Dollop a good sized tablespoon of buttercream or cream cheese frosting (this will not work with ganache or meringue) on top of each of your cupcakes. You want to leave a small mound in the middle of each one. (**A**)

2 Knead and prepare your sugarpaste for rolling (see page 35), adding any colour if required, and roll out with your rolling pin, using marzipan spacers to ensure an even thickness. (**B**)

3 Cut out 12 circles from this sugarpaste using the round cookie cutter. To cover your cupcake, gently lay a circle of sugarpaste over the top of each buttercream-topped cake. Be careful not to press on the centre of your sugarpaste, instead use your fingers to gently tease down the edges of the sugarpaste circle to the edges of your cupcake. (**C**)

4 Once the sugarpaste has formed a dome over the buttercream and you are confident that it is securely contained, cup your hand and give a gentle turn over the top of your covered cupcake. The heat from your palm will create a beautifully smooth finish. (**D**)

A

B

Covering a Large Cake in Sugarpaste

1 x levelled, filled and crumb-coated cake
    (see pages 26–29), fridge-cold
sugar syrup (made by dissolving 2 tablespoons
    caster/granulated sugar in 2 tablespoons
    boiling water, set aside to cool)
1 kg/2¼ lbs. sugarpaste for a 20-cm/8-in.
    cake and 750 g/1⅔ lbs. for a 15-cm/
    6-in. cake
cornflour/cornstarch, for dusting

pastry brush
40-cm/16-in. non-stick rolling pin (or larger)
marzipan spacers
pizza wheel
straight-edge smoother
ribbon
ruler

Sugarpaste is the most common icing used to cover celebration cakes. It is also known as 'fondant' icing in the US or 'ready to roll' icing and is made from a mixture of sugar and glucose. Not all sugarpastes are equal so it is worth experimenting with different brands to find a taste you enjoy and a texture that you can work with. This technique is the foundation of great cake design. Practice will always make perfect so do not rush it! Remember that sugarpaste needs to be thoroughly warmed through to make it pliable enough to place on or fold over the top edges of your cake comfortably.

1 Brush the entire surface of your cooled crumb-coated cake – top and sides – with sugar syrup. Though the cake needs to be cold and set to work with, it also needs to be sticky for the sugarpaste to adhere. Ensure that you brush every part of the cake as dry patches can lead to air pockets appearing. Set the cake aside while preparing the sugarpaste.

2 Knead your sugarpaste on a clean surface (see box on page 35) (**A**). If you are adding colour to white sugarpaste, it should be kneaded through now. Only use paste or gel colours, never a liquid colour, as they will not affect the consistency of the icing. Add colour a little at a time using a cocktail stick/toothpick (you can always add more colour but it is far harder to take it away).

3 Once you are happy that your sugarpaste is warmed through and malleable, dust your work surface with cornflour/cornstarch and press your ball of sugarpaste – smooth-side-up – down into a large flat disc. This will save you a good few minutes of rolling out.

4 Lay your marzipan spacers either side of your sugarpaste on their lowest height setting.

5 Use your non-stick rolling pin to roll out your sugarpaste in long, fluid strokes (**B**). When your sugarpaste is fully rolled out and your rolling pin has reached the top of your spacers, check that you have rolled out a large enough circle to cover your cake.

6 Lift your sugarpaste onto your cake (**C**). If you are confident doing this by rolling the paste over your rolling pin, then go for it! I prefer to slide my hands and forearms underneath my sugarpaste, fingers flat and together so that my hands are flat paddles. With my arms in the centre of my sugarpaste, I can lift quite safely and securely. Using your arms as a centre point, lift your sugarpaste to just above your cake until your arms are in line with the centre and gently remove your arms out to either side, allowing the icing to fall onto the surface of the cake between your arms.

7 Work your hand around the sides of your cake, starting at the top edges and working your way to the bottom, always smoothing in upwards strokes (**D**). Smoothing downwards can put stress on your sugarpaste and cause cracks and tears. You will know that you are done when you can feel the work surface beneath your hand. (**E**)

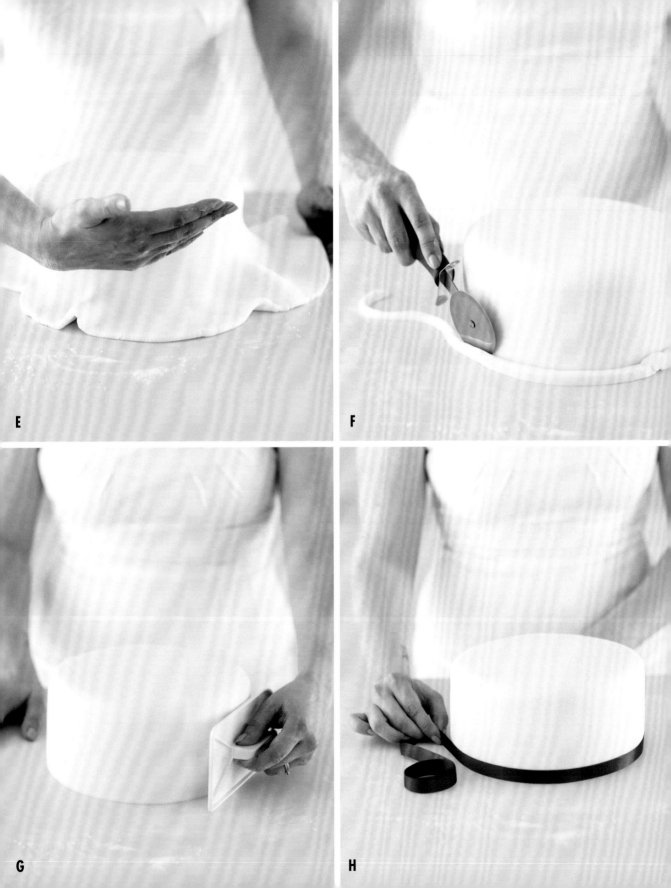

E

F

G

H

8 Leave roughly 2.5 cm/1 in. of excess sugarpaste around the bottom of the cake, then cut away any remaining sugarpaste using a pizza wheel. Press the 2.5 cm/1 in. excess sugarpaste into the bottom edge of your cake using the lower edge of your palm until you can see a distinct line running between the excess sugarpaste and the cake – this is your 'cut here' guide line. By knocking the sugarpaste into the bottom edge of the cake, you will ensure perfect thickness of paste from the top of your cake down. Be bold and run your pizza wheel into this guide line all around your cake. (**F**)

9 Use your straight-edge smoother as a little iron to smooth out the surface of your sugarpaste. With the long straight edge of your smoother flush against your work surface and the paddle of the smoother gently pressed against your cake, work your way around the cake 2–3 times and over the top. Don't overdo this as the sugarpaste will start to dry and you could end up causing the cracks that you have worked so hard to avoid. (**G**)

10 I recommend that you leave your perfectly covered cake overnight before dowelling, stacking or decorating, in this case with a gorgeous red ribbon around the bottom (**H**). The reason that professional cake designers do this is to allow the sugarpaste time to 'crust over' or dry enough to enable us to handle the cake without fear of causing damage with rogue fingerprints!

Tips for Working with Sugarpaste

Knead to Know
By investing a little time in kneading your sugarpaste, you can prevent the appearance of tiny cracks around the top edge and ensure a smooth finish. Sugarpaste does not need to be pulled around in the same way as bread does. Knead your sugarpaste around in a tight ball – this will warm your paste sufficiently and you should find that all folds and creases in your paste are on the top of your ball, while the bottom part against the work surface is perfectly smooth.

Follow the Formula
To work out how much sugarpaste you'll need to fit a cake, follow a simple formula: **Cake diameter + (height x 2) = sugarpaste diameter**. So, for a 20-cm/8-in. cake with a 10-cm/4-in. height (or drop), you'll need a circle of sugarpaste with a 40-cm/16-in. diameter. Before rolling out the sugarpaste, you'll need to use marzipan spacers, which act as a guide to rolling out the sugarpaste to a uniform thickness. Marzipan spacers should always be within the length of your rolling pin to guarantee an even thickness of sugarpaste. You have finished rolling out when your rolling pin reaches the top of these spacers.

On a Roll
Get into the discipline of rolling once forward (in one long movement that goes from hands, to wrists, to forearms), then once back, and then turning your sugarpaste by a quarter turn. This will ensure that you are getting an even roll and that you notice any sticking to the work surface as soon as possible. If you find that your sugarpaste is starting to stick, just throw a small amount of cornflour/cornstarch underneath, keep calm, and carry on.

Smooth Operator
If the sugarpaste is forming folds and creases around the sides of your cake, don't panic. Treat it like fabric and open up any folds with one hand, smoothing the paste back onto your cake with an upward stroke from your free hand.

Dowelling & Stacking for Tiered Cakes

Creating tiered cakes requires a little structural engineering. The idea behind dowelling is that each cake rests upon a construction of dowelling rods rather than on the cake below. Once you have mastered this technique, the sky is (quite literally) the limit!

parchment circle the same size as the cake you wish to stack on top of a larger cake
ruler
pencil
spirit level
4 bamboo dowelling rods
junior hacksaw
small palette knife

1 Fold your parchment circle into quarters. Based on dowelling an 20-cm/8-in. cake to support a 15-cm/6-in. cake, you will need a 15-cm/6-in. parchment circle. By folding quarters, you will now have an accurate guide for placing four dowelling rods into your cake. Lay your parchment circle centrally on top of your cake and mark a point 2.5 cm/1 in. from the edge along each guide line.

2 If you are working with a sugarpaste cake, use your spirit level to check if any of these points is higher than the others. If you do have a highest point, push your first dowelling rod straight down into your cake at this point until the rod reaches the bottom. If you do not have a highest point, or if you are working with a cake that is not covered with sugarpaste, just pick any one.

3 Make a pencil mark on your dowelling rod a millimetre or two just above the line of your icing. This is now your measurement for your remaining three dowelling rods. Gently twist as you pull this first dowelling rod up and out of your cake, preventing any damage to the icing. (**A**)

4 Cut your 4 dowelling rods to the pencil mark that you made on the first rod (**B**). The reason that we measure all four rods from this one measurement is that it is unlikely that your cake will be 100% level all over. What appears straight to the naked eye may well cause problems in construction – I'm sure someone looked at the Tower of Pisa and thought it looked fine!

5 Check, check and check again that your four dowelling rods are now equal lengths. Once you are happy, insert your original dowelling rod carefully back into the hole that you have already made before inserting each dowelling rod into the points marked on top of your cake. (**C**)

6 You should find that your dowels are visible and slightly raised from the surface of your cake. You may notice that some rods appear to stick further up from your cake than others – this is only a measure of the surface of your cake and further evidence why measuring your dowels in this way is far more reliable than using the cake itself!

7 For sugarpaste-covered cakes, using a little 'gloop' made from left over sugarpaste, heated for 30 seconds in a microwave, seal your dowelling rods in place by pressing the gloop on top of them with a small palette knife. For any other type of cake, just use a little excess buttercream, ganache or frosting. Leave a small blob at the top of each dowelling rod.

8 Carefully lift your smaller tier on top of your dowelled tier. Take your time. Ensure that your top cake is central and secure. Leave the cake to set firm for at least an hour before you consider moving it. (**D**)

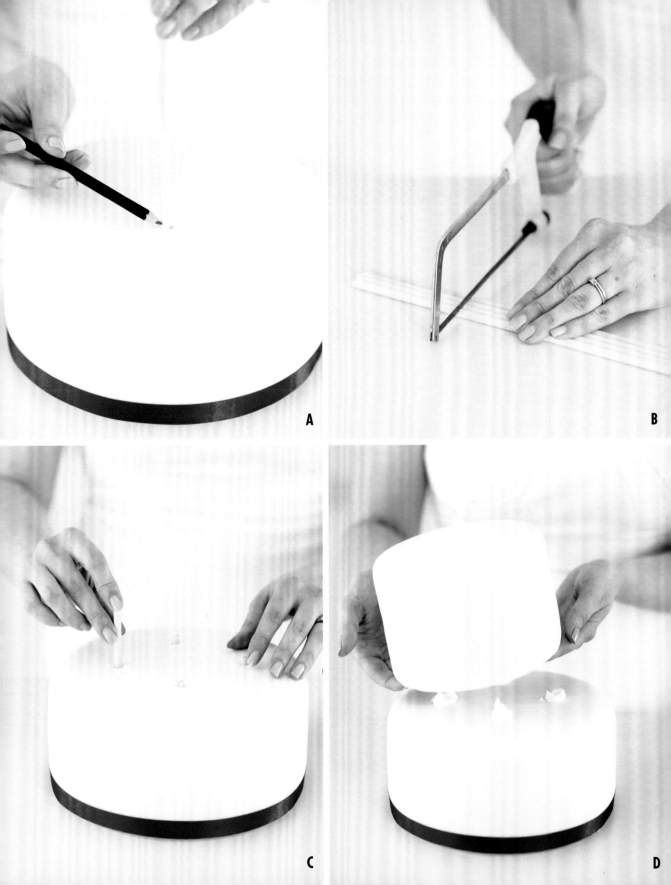

A

B

C

D

Royal Icing Piping Techniques

Royal icing is a mixture of fine sugar and egg albumen, which lends an elasticity to the icing – allowing it to be stretched as it is piped with greater control. The strength of this icing means that it can be piped into very fine and delicate patterns as well as larger ones.

1 egg white per 250 g/9 oz. icing/confectioners'
    sugar (if making larger quantities, continue in this ratio)
1–2 drops lemon juice

Beat the egg white and the sugar together with the lemon juice on high speed in a free-standing mixer for 10 minutes. Alternatively, you can use packeted royal icing, which I actually prefer. To prepare packeted icing, you just need to add water and beat for 10 minutes on full speed in a free-standing mixer. You may need to beat for longer if using an electric hand whisk, but note that you won't be able to mix the correct consistency by hand. Your royal icing is ready to pipe when it can hold a peak that folds over slightly at the top. Ideally, you should stop whisking as soon as the icing is at this stage to prevent it becoming too dry with over-whisking. At ideal consistency, your royal icing will be stiff enough to hold shape beautifully but wet enough to pipe smoothly.

Fitting a piping bag

I always use disposable piping bags to pipe my royal icing in order to avoid washing up the reusable ones. My preference is to use plastic piping bags for larger piping jobs, where there is a benefit in having a sturdy piping bag, and parchment triangles for smaller, more intricate work where I need a more comfortable grip. You can buy ready-cut parchment triangles for piping or cut your own from baking parchment.

1 Cut a triangle with 1 long edge across the top and 2 shorter edges beneath – roll the top 2 corners of the long edge down to meet the point at the bottom of your triangle to make a cone shape (**A**), folding the points inside the cone to secure them. (**B**)

2 Drop a piping nozzle/tip into your piping bag.

3 Fill the bag with 2–3 tablespoons of royal icing. Fold the piping bag back over so that you form a triangular shape at the top containing the icing (**C**); roll the excess bag down and you are ready to pipe (**D**).

Practice makes perfect

When it comes to royal icing, I'm afraid you will need to practice. You can photocopy the template on page 159 to help you!

Dots: Using a small round nozzle/tip, held still directly above and almost (but not) touching the paper, squeeze your piping bag gently until the icing has covered the black dot on the template. When you are happy with the size of your dot, stop squeezing and pull your nozzle/tip up and away from the dot. If you find that there is a small peak, this can be flattened using a very slightly damp paintbrush.

Lines: Using a small round nozzle/tip, held still directly above and almost (but not) touching the paper the paper, squeeze your piping bag gently until the icing has made contact with one end of the black line. Continue squeezing gently but lift your nozzle/tip a little higher so that an unbroken line of icing is falling onto the paper. You will need to keep an eye on where your icing is falling and think ahead to the point at which you will need to stop squeezing the bag and bring your piping nozzle/tip back down to connect with the end point of the line. By using gravity in this way, you will always achieve a smoother line.

Circles: Using a small round nozzle/tip, held still directly above and almost (but not) touching the paper the paper, squeeze your piping bag gently until the icing has made contact with the top of the circle. The method is the same as piping lines, with your nozzle/tip raised a little higher than the paper and your icing falling onto the circle, but you will need to take your time when moving through 7–9 o'clock (if you are going clockwise) as this is the trickiest bit! When you reach 10 o'clock, stop piping and bring your nozzle/tip with the trail of icing down to rest at 12 o'clock.

Congratulations, you can now pipe pretty much anything!

Stencilling Techniques

Stencilling is a great way to add intricate detailing to your cakes. Made of durable food-grade plastic, stencils are available in a wide range of designs and patterns —though you may need to search online to find them. Fiddly but ultimately fantastic you will need practice to master these techniques, or an extra hand or two!

cake stencil
length of ribbon
sticky tape
small palette knife
paintbrush

1 Line your cake stencil up against the side of your 20-cm/8-in. cake (**A**). Wrap a length of spare ribbon around the bottom of the cake to set the stencil higher if required or use a little sticky tape to stick either end of the stencil to the cake. Take your time to get your stencil exactly where you want it to be.

2 Take a small blob of royal icing on a palette knife and gently press this on top of your stencil (**B**). This is important – you do not want to push the royal icing into the stencil or start spreading it back and forth onto the stencil as it will just go underneath the plastic and make a mess. Go slowly, working with a small amount each time until you have covered your stencil (**C**).

3 Clean off your palette knife and angle it against your stencil so that the blade runs straight down the entire length of the stencil. Pull your palette knife along the side of the stencil to remove the excess royal icing. You may need to make 2–3 scrapes to do the whole length of the stencil.

4 Once you are happy that the excess has been removed, carefully pull your stencil away from the side of your cake. Hold both ends of the stencil and pull towards you to minimise any spreading of the icing beneath.

5 You will now be able to see if there are any smudges in your design. If there are any mistakes, these can be cleared up using a damp paintbrush (**D**).

6 The stencil that I have used for this pattern is one standalone pattern, with no need to line up the stencil to repeat the pattern. If you are working with a repeated pattern, you will need to wait 5–10 minutes for your last stencilled area to dry, then line up your stencil correctly to continue the pattern and repeat steps 1–5.

A

B

C

D

Seasons & Celebrations

Spring: Day of the Peonies Cake

20-cm/8-in. Lemon Drizzle Cake (see page 15), crumb-coated (see pages 26–29) with Basic Buttercream coloured pale yellow (see page 20)

50 g/1½ oz. sugarpaste

3 Sugar Peonies (see pages 46–47), coloured pale pink using Claret food colouring paste

large piping bag fitted with a large 1 cm/³⁄₈ in. round piping nozzle/tip
small palette knife

Serves up to 20

I'm lucky enough have peonies in my garden. They bloom beautifully for about one day each May before exploding all over the lawn. Nevertheless, they are stunning, bright and scented, and I look forward to my own 'day of the peonies' each spring.

1 Prepare and crumb-coat your Lemon Drizzle Cake. Fill your piping bag (see pages 38–39) with the pale yellow buttercream and use this to pipe a vertical line of dots, with a diameter of approximately 2 cm/³⁄₄ in. each, down the side of your chilled cake. You can either use a large round piping nozzle/tip for this design or simply cut the end of a disposable piping nozzle/tip to required size.

2 Use your palette knife to drag each dot of buttercream into a scallop shape. Hold your knife horizontally with the blade laid flat and pressed gently into the middle of the dot. Drag the buttercream beneath your blade to the right until the line trails off.

3 Pipe another vertical line of dots over the point at which the last dots began to disappear and repeat step 2. You should now see how each line will build up to create this scalloped pattern.

4 Repeat this process until your entire cake is covered, finishing with a final vertical line of neat buttercream dots at the back of your cake. Cakes often have a 'back' and this is a nice way to finish off your design.

5 Roll a small ball of sugarpaste and place this centrally on top of your cake.

6 Trim the wires of your Sugar Peonies to around 3 cm/1 in. long. Arrange your peonies on top of the cake, with their wires pressed into the ball of sugarpaste to hold them securely.

A

B

C

Sugar Peonies

300 g/10½ oz. flower paste (remember to knead your paste to warm through before rolling it out)

a little green flower paste

5-cm/2-in. polystyrene ball
ball tool or a cocktail stick/toothpick
20-gauge floristry wire (green or white)
non-stick board
small non-stick rolling pin
set of peony petal cutters
foam mat
edible glue
small paintbrush
a glass
tissue paper
small 5-petal rose cutter
green floristry tape

The peonies that I make are big, blousy and make quite a statement, although they are made using a very simple process and a single set of peony cutters.

1 Push a cocktail stick/toothpick horizontally through the middle of your polystyrene ball to create a tunnel for you to push your wire through. Use a whole length of wire and, with your bud at the centre, pull both ends of the wire down and twist them into one double-strength wire. This is the centre of your peony.

2 On a non-stick board, knead and roll out enough flower paste to cut 4 pieces using your medium-sized peony petal cutter. Transfer these petals to your foam mat and use a ball tool or a cocktail stick/toothpick to 'frill' the top edges of each petal. To do this, lay your ball tool or cocktail stick/toothpick against the top edge of your petal and roll back and forth until the petals become thinner and appear to have movement. (**A**)

3 Paint each petal with a little edible glue from around half way down to the very bottom. Lay your first 2 petals opposite each other at the top of your ball so that the second overlaps the top of the first. Turn your ball by a quarter turn. Lay your third and fourth petals opposite each other on the ball but leave them open so that you can look down to the first and second petals below. (**B**)

4 Cut 10 small peony petals and frill them in the same way as outlined in step 2. Stick these petals around the sides of your ball with edible glue on the back, each one slightly overlapping the last. Be mindful of movement and use your fingers to adjust any petals that look a little close together. (**C**)

5 Cut another 14 petals using your medium-sized peony petal cutter, frill the edges and add them to the ball following the technique you used in step 4. It's best to leave your peony to dry after adding this layer to prevent the weight of the paste pulling the soft petals off the ball. (**D**)

E

F

6 Cut another 14 petals using your largest peony petal cutter and repeat step 4 again. If you wish to create a larger, more open peony, allow to dry and then add another layer (**E**)

7 Once you are happy with the size of your peony, leave it to dry the right way up, standing in something that will support its shape, like a glass (**F**). Lay a few layers of tissue paper over the top of the glass and poke the stem of your peony through the centre. Once the peony is secure, use smaller pieces of tissue paper to add movement to your petals by pushing small pieces between layers of your petals.

8 Once dry, finish your peony with a calyx made using green flower paste and a small 5-petal rose cutter (**G**). Frill the edges of the calyx with a ball tool, paint a dab of edible glue on the middle, and push your wire through the centre. Leave to dry.

9 Trim your wire to the length you need it to be and wrap with green floristry wire to create a stem. To create a realistic, thicker stem, wrap a small length of tissue paper around your wire before you tape it.

G

Summer: Eton Mess Cake

20-cm/8-in. Classic Victoria
  Sponge Cake (see page 14)
  filled with Vanilla
  Buttercream (see page 20)
  and strawberry jam

Marshmallow Meringue
  Frosting (see page 23)

fresh strawberries

meringues (store-bought nests
  are fine for this)

double/heavy cream or clotted
  cream, to serve

Serves up to 20

Nothing says 'Great British Summertime' like Eton Mess. This is my homage to warm summer days filled with ripe strawberries, whipped cream and meringue in cake form! This cake would be the perfect centrepiece to any garden party and is best enjoyed at the height of summer with friends.

1 Prepare your Victoria Sponge Cake, filled with Vanilla Buttercream and strawberry jam. I would recommend that you prepare this cake to be eaten on the same day to enjoy it at its best.

2 Cover the cake with Marshmallow Meringue Frosting. I have chosen to straighten the edges of my frosting using the same techniques as described on pages 26–29, but you could adopt a more rustic approach if you like.

3 Decorate with beautifully ripe, fresh strawberries. I've used halved strawberries with a few whole ones to decorate the centre. Be careful to dry your strawberries thoroughly after washing them to avoid any rogue moisture escaping and dissolving your frosting.

4 Crumble your meringues into a bowl, gathering a mismatched rubble of larger lumps and finer pieces. Scatter these broken shards of meringue on top of your cake and allow the pieces to distribute themselves organically. Part of the charm of this design comes from its slightly cavalier appearance.

5 Serve alfresco on a sunny day with lashings of double/heavy cream or a cheeky dollop of clotted cream.

Autumn: Golden Leaves Cake

20-cm/8-in. Chocolate Mud Cake (see page 17) filled with Chocolate Buttercream (see page 20) and covered with Dark Chocolate Ganache (see page 22)

100 g/3½ oz. dark modelling chocolate mixed with ½ teaspoon CMC powder

100 g/3½ oz. milk modelling chocolate mixed with ½ teaspoon CMC powder

edible gold lustre spray

cornflour/cornstarch, for dusting

non-stick board

small non-stick rolling pin

rose leaf plunger cutters in different sizes

Serves up to 20

As a child of the autumn, I find that the turning of the leaves each year is especially exciting. I love that the evening sunlight takes on a golden hue, and the cooling air makes it acceptable to bring out those long leather gloves again. Though I understand that not everyone shares my enthusiasm for the colder evenings, I think we can all agree that there is nothing so satisfying as a pile of fallen leaves, all brown and crisp, just begging to be jumped into... well, nothing except for a chocolate cake perhaps!

1 Prepare your Chocolate Mud Cake with a filling of Chocolate Buttercream and cover with a thick layer of Dark Chocolate Ganache.

2 To make the chocolate leaves for this cake, roll out dark modelling chocolate to around 3 mm/ ⅛ in. thickness and cut out a selection of leaves using plunger cutters (see pages 52–53). You will find that plunger cutters are the quickest and most convenient method for creating realistic looking leaves. Simply cut out your shape, press the plunger down once on your work surface to indent the veined detail on your leaf, and then press the plunger again above your work surface allowing the leaf to fall out. Alternatively, use templates and a small sharp knife.

3 Repeat step 2 with your milk modelling chocolate.

4 Allow your chocolate leaves to dry for at least 2 hours on a crumpled sheet of baking parchment, so that they dry with an impression of movement.

5 Once your chocolate leaves are dry, give them a quick spray with the edible gold lustre spray to make them shine.

6 Assemble a cascade of leaves onto your cake, using a little reserved chocolate ganache as the glue to stick them on. Start at the bottom of your cake and build upwards so that higher leaves can rest on lower ones. You may need to do this in 2–3 stages to allow the supporting leaves to adhere securely before building on them.

Simple Blossoms & Leaves

sugarpaste mixed with CMC powder (1 teaspoon per 250 g/9 oz. of sugarpaste), coloured as appropriate (I recommend using sugarpaste mixed with CMC for these flowers as they are small and do not need to be wired so are perfectly edible)

non-stick board

small non-stick rolling pin

cornflour/cornstarch, for dusting

There are some fantastic products on the market which will enable you to make beautifully crafted flowers and leaves quickly, and with minimal fuss.

Plunger cutters: great for producing lots of tiny blossoms from cutters that would be impractical without the addition of the plunger to remove the tiny shape. To use a plunger cutter:

1 Dip the cutter section in a little cornflour/cornstarch and then press down on the plunger to dust this area too and ensure that it will not get stuck to your sugarpaste.

2 Roll out your sugarpaste to around 2 mm/$^{1}/_{16}$ in. thickness and cut out a shape using only the cutter, being careful not to press on the plunger (**A**). Lift your cutter away then press down on the plunger to eject the shape (**B**). Some plunger cutters have a built-in veiner which adds detail. You'll need to first cut out the shape, press down the plunger once on a flat surface to add the detail, before plunging a second time to eject the shape.

Cutter and mould sets: I am a big fan of these for creating quick and detailed flowers. To use them:

1 Roll out your sugarpaste to around 2 mm/$^{1}/_{16}$ in. thickness and cut out the shape of your flower with the cutter. Before you remove the shape, give the cutter a little rub on your foam mat to tidy up any edges that may be a little rough.

2 Remove your flower shape from the cutter and lay it inside the mould that matches the shape of your cutter (**C**) – dust a little cornflour/cornstarch on both sides of the mould first. Close the mould with the flower shape inside, press gently, and then open to reveal your beautifully detailed flower (**D**). Leave these flowers to dry on crumpled baking parchment to preserve their open shape.

Silicone moulds: come in all shapes and sizes and are extremely quick to use. To use silicone moulds:

1 Dust the inside liberally with cornflour/cornstarch and turn it upside down to shake away the excess

2 Take a ball of sugarpaste (mixed with CMC) that is slightly smaller than the mould you want to fill and press the paste down until it has covered the entire shape (**E**), turn the mould over and tap to release (**F**).

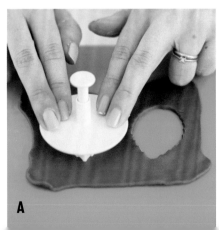

A

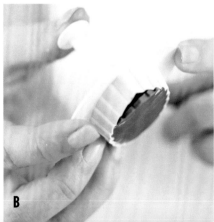

B

C

D

E

F

Winter: Frosted Wonderland Cake

20-cm/8-in. Salted Caramel
   Cake (see page 18) filled
   with Salted Caramel
   Buttercream (see page 20)
   and covered with White
   Chocolate Ganache (see
   page 22)
100 g/3½ oz. white
   modelling chocolate
cornflour/cornstarch, for
   dusting
edible silver lustre spray
silver dragees

silver ribbon
non-stick board
small non-stick rolling pin
snowflake plunger cutters (see
   pages 52–53)

Serves up to 20

Though the winter days may be cold and short, they can be beautiful and sparkling, particularly when snow is involved. The romance in freshly fallen snowflakes is something I've tried to recreate in this design.

1 Prepare your Salted Caramel Cake with a filling of Salted Caramel Buttercream and cover with a layer of White Chocolate Ganache, reserving a little for later.

2 Once you're happy that you have a nice thick, even covering of white chocolatey ganache on your cake, smooth around the edges and straighten the top using the technique on pages 26–29.

3 On a non-stick board using a small non-stick rolling pin, roll out your white modelling chocolate to around 3 mm/⅛ in. thickness and cut snowflakes from this in a variety of sizes. I have used a set of snowflake plunger cutters which have a built-in veiner to add a little detail to each shape. You will need to cut approximately 30–40 snowflakes to complete this design. Leave these to dry for at least 2 hours on a flat surface.

4 Spray your white chocolate snowflakes with a little edible silver lustre spray (not forgetting to give the can a thorough shake before you use it) and begin to arrange snowflakes on top of your cake, using a little reserved white chocolate ganache as your glue.

5 To create the illusion of snowflakes falling and settling on your cake, concentrate your snowflakes on the top of your cake, allowing some to overlap, and falling down just over the top edges. Reserve your very smallest snowflakes to look as if they are falling down the sides of your cake.

6 Finish this design with a few silver dragees, pressed into the white chocolate ganache covering of your cake, to add a little extra seasonal sparkle.

Valentine's Day Gift Box

20-cm/8-in. Chocolate Mud Cake (see page 17) filled with Chocolate Buttercream and crumb-coated (see pages 26–29) with Vanilla Buttercream (see page 20)

1.5 kg/3¼ lbs sugarpaste, coloured pale pink

2 tablespoons CMC powder

480 g/1 lb. sugarpaste, coloured dark pink

20 g/¾ oz. sugarpaste, white

black food colouring

chocolate truffles (or your choice of chocolates)

metallic gold food paint

small paintbrush
marzipan spacers
30-cm/12-in. ruler
pizza wheel

Serves up to 20

This is a design for all you romantic souls out there wanting to bake up something delicious for someone special.

1 Cover the prepared Chocolate Mud Cake using 1 kg/2¼ lbs of pale pink sugarpaste (see pages 32–35).

2 Knead the CMC powder into the remaining 500 g/1 lb. of pale pink sugarpaste. Roll this sugarpaste out, using your marzipan spacers as a thickness guide, and cut around the 20-cm/8-in. pan that you baked your cake in. Set this circle of sugarpaste aside to dry on a flat surface for at least 8 hours. You can continue to decorate this circle, which will become your box lid, while it dries.

3 Roll out your dark pink sugarpaste into a length around 5 mm/¼ in. thick. I like to use a 30-cm/12-in. ruler as a measure for the width of the strip that I want to cut from this sugarpaste, so lay your ruler on top of the paste and cut along both long edges with a pizza wheel. Your strip will need to be 20 cm/8 in. long.

4 Paint a scant line of water across the middle of your pale pink lid and lay this first strip of dark pink sugarpaste along the line. Trim the edges of this strip so that they line up with the circle of sugarpaste. Repeat step 3 but this time, cut your 20-cm/8-in. strip into two 10-cm/4-in. strips and cut a triangle from one end of each. These will now become the tails of your sugarpaste bow. Dab a little water at the top and bottom of each tail and position these at the centre of your box lid, on top of your long dark pink strip.

5 Repeat step 3 but this time, cut a 30-cm/12-in. length of sugarpaste and divide into two 15 cm/6 in. lengths. These will form the ribbon loops of your bow. Curl these lengths into 2 large teardrop shapes and position them at the centre of your box lid to create the illusion of a hand-tied bow. Press the outer edges of your bow loops gently towards the centre of the bow to create a fatter looking bow.

6 Repeat step 3 but this time, roll a short length of only 7.5 cm/3 in. to create the centre of your bow. You will need to measure this centre part against your bow and trim any excess away. Once you are happy that this section will fit, paint its back with a little water and press into position.

7 Roll out your white sugarpaste to around 3 mm/⅛ in. thickness and cut into the shape of a gift tag. Cut a small hole at the top of your tag using a large round piping nozzle/tip and thread a thin sausage of dark pink sugarpaste through to create a tie. Use black food colouring on a fine paintbrush to write a little message to your loved one, allowing this to dry before fixing the tag to the top of your lid with a tiny dab of water.

8 Roll a long thin sausage of pale pink sugarpaste, approximately 66 cm/26 in. long, and lay this around the top edge of your cake, securing with a little water.

9 Paint half of the top of your cake with gold metallic food paint and then arrange your chocolates to cover this half, going right up to the lip that you have created around the edge. Position your box lid carefully on top of your cake so that the lid rests on the chocolates, giving the recipient a little peak inside!

Fabergé Easter Egg Cookies

12 Basic Cookies (see page 19), but cut using an egg-shaped cookie cutter

250 g/1⅓ cups royal icing

gold dragees

assorted paste or gel food colouring in jewel shades (I have used Royal Blue, Red Extra, Grape Violet, and Green)

gold metallic food paint

cocktail stick/toothpick
parchment piping bag fitted with a small round nozzle/tip (one for each colour of icing)
squeezy plastic bottle (one for each colour of icing)
small paintbrush

Makes 12

Oh, how I love beautiful enamelled eggs! For so long I have admired their intricate detailing and stunning colours but, to this day, I still have no idea what on earth they are for. Perhaps part of their appeal is that they exist only to be beautiful and admired, with no function or other purpose than this, and that is enough for me. Personally, I think that these cookies make the most glamorous Easter gift. They are deceptively inexpensive to make and easy to make truly personal.

1 Mix up your royal icing until it holds stiff peaks before dividing between as many bowls as you wish to create colours for your cookies. Add the colour using a cocktail stick/toothpick to each bowl. I recommend leaving one bowl white. Ensure that any royal icing you are not using is covered with clingfilm/plastic wrap to prevent it from drying out.

2 For each colour, spoon 2–3 tablespoons of stiff icing into a parchment piping bag fitted with a small round nozzle/tip.

3 Pipe a line of icing around the top edge of each cookie. This technique of icing cookies is known as 'flooding' so you are, in effect, piping a 'floodgate' that will contain the icing neatly on top of your cookie.

4 Add sufficient cold water to the coloured icing remaining in your bowls to change the consistency from stiff icing to 'seven-second' icing. This is so-called, because you are aiming for a runny consistency where a spoon removed in the middle of stirring the icing will leave a ripple that disappears in the count of seven, leaving a perfectly flat surface. I recommend pouring this icing into squeezy plastic bottles — you will thank me!

5 Squeeze your runny icing on top of your cookies, filling up the cookie but leaving a 5 mm/¼ in. gap from the floodgate line of icing so that your runny icing has space to settle into. Once you are happy that you have squeezed sufficient icing onto your cookie, set your squeezy bottle aside and gently tease your runny icing to the floodgate line using a cocktail stick/toothpick. Leave your cookies to dry overnight.

6 Fill a parchment piping bag fitted with a small round nozzle/tip with a little stiff white royal icing and use this to pipe details onto your cookies (see pages 38–39). Think swirling flourishes and geometric lines, taking your inspiration from over 100 years of Fabergé egg designs. Add gold, silver and pearl dragees for extra sparkle.

7 Allow your white piped details to dry for at least 1 hour before painting carefully with gold metallic food paint. Present these to your loved ones for a truly eggs-travagant (sorry!) Easter gift.

Mother's Day & Father's Day Cupcakes

12 cupcakes in the flavour of your choice (see pages 14–18), covered with sugarpaste (see pages 30–31)

250 g/9 oz. sugarpaste

1 teaspoon CMC powder

assorted paste or gel food colouring (I've used Sky Blue and Claret)

gold dragees

non-stick board
small non-stick rolling pin
pizza wheel and a sharp knife
OR a bow cutter (I have used a selection by JEM cutters)
small paintbrush

Makes 12

Baking books tend to favour Mother's Day when it comes to sweet offerings, but I think that fathers deserve a little treat on Father's Day too. What gift could be sweeter than cupcakes? This is a simple way of creating beautifully elegant cupcakes, guaranteed to impress the sternest of parents! And why not add your mum or dad's favourite colour instead of the ones I have suggested, to make it even more personal.

1 Begin by covering your cupcakes with sugarpaste using the technique on pages 30–31, and add your choice of colour using a cocktail stick/toothpick. I have used Sky Blue for my two designs to create a Tiffany-inspired cake for my mum and a cake inspired by my father's favourite soccer team.

2 To make sugar bows, knead the CMC powder into the sugarpaste and add colour if you wish. I have added Claret colouring to Dad's half of the sugarpaste and left Mum's white.

3 Follow the technique on pages 62–63 to make the sugar bows for your Mother's Day Cupcakes. If you are making Father' Day Cupcakes, lay your bow tails horizontally with a little movement in them as we did for the Mother's Day cupcakes. Then, with a dab of water at the middle of the tails, lay your bow on top of the tails. Press gently on the outer edges of your bow to push them in towards the middle to create that classic bow tie shape.

4 Finish the Father's Day Cupcakes by adding 3 gold dragees to recreate the look of buttons running down a shirt. Then, why not find a little box to present them in, lined with some coloured tissue paper.

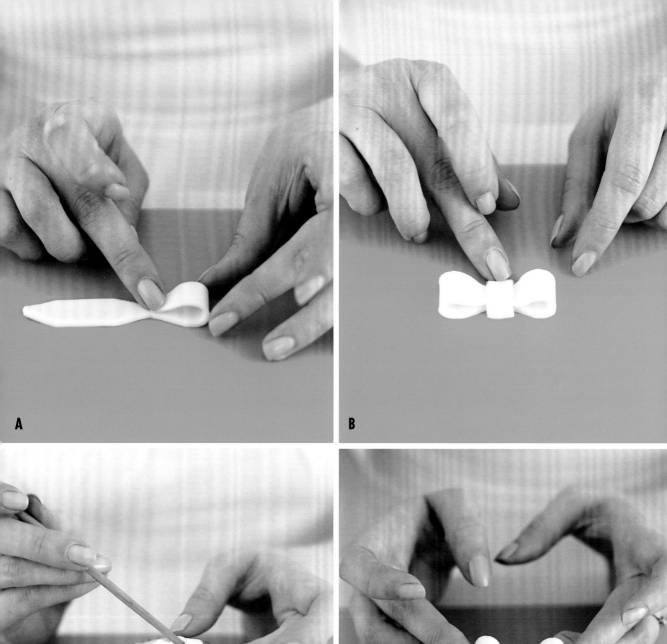

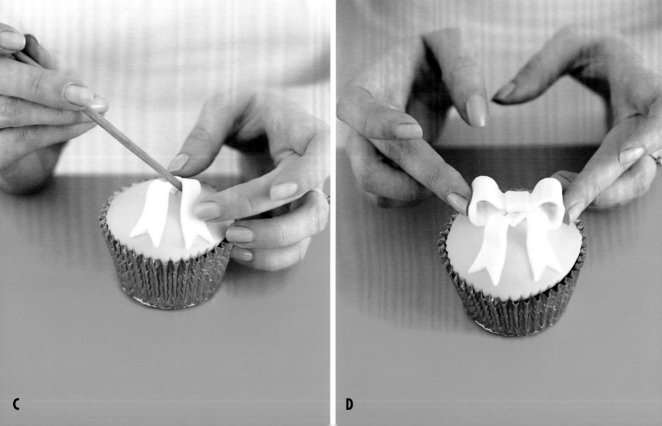

A

B

C

D

Sugar Bows

250 g/9 oz. sugarpaste, mixed with 1 teaspoon CMC powder

non-stick board

small non-stick rolling pin
bow cutter (I have used one by JEM) OR a pizza wheel and a small knife
small paintbrush

Sugar bows really are the perfect way to tie up any cake or cupcake. Arranged en masse either on a beautiful platter or – even better – a cupcake tower, these simple decorations can prove just as breathtaking as elaborate sugar flowers.

1 Roll out your sugarpaste to around 3 mm/⅛ in. thick and cut out the sections that you will need to assemble your bow. You can either use a cutter for this, as I have, which will cut out uniform-sized pieces for each bow, or you can cut freehand using a pizza wheel (see step 2). I have used a medium bow cutter by JEM (these are available in smaller and larger versions).

2 To cut a freehand sugar bow, use your pizza wheel to cut a strip 8 cm/3 in. long and 1 cm/⅜ in. wide. Cut this strip in half and use your knife to cut a triangle from the bottom end of each piece. These now become the tails of your bow.

3 Cut a second strip 10 cm/4 in. long and 1 cm/⅜ in. wide. With a tiny dab of water in its centre, bring both ends of the strip into the middle to form the ribbon loops of your bow (**A**). Cut a small strip of sugarpaste and press this over the central join, wrapping it around to secure underneath the bow so that your ribbon appears to be tied in one long strip (**B**).

4 To assemble your bow, first arrange your bow tails on top of your cupcake (**C**) or onto baking parchment. Bring your ribbon tails into a V-shape with the tops of the tails overlapping. Use a tiny dab of water to secure this overlapped section. Create movement in the tails by gently teasing them into folds with your paintbrush.

5 Dab a little water at the top of your ribbon tails and carefully lay your ribbon loops on top. Press gently on the outer edges of your loops (**D**) to create movement. This is your bow.

A Midsummer Night's Dream Cake

20-cm/8-in. and 15-cm/6-in. Lemon Drizzle Cake tiers (see page 15)

1.5 kg/3¼ lbs sugarpaste, coloured pale green (I have used Mint Green)

500 g/1 lb 2 oz. sugarpaste mixed with 2 teaspoons CMC powder (divided into 4 portions and coloured dark purple, violet, pale yellow and white)

100 g/3½ oz. dark green sugarpaste mixed with ½ teaspoon CMC powder

125 g/²⁄₃ cup royal icing

Hologram White edible glitter

selection of flower cutter and mould sets — I have used hydrangea, buttercup, cherry blossom, primula and snow rose
leaf cutters and moulds
4 dowelling rods
gold ribbon
small palette knife

Serves up to 34

In various parts of the world, the feast of Midsummer is still celebrated — the magical longest day at which summer reaches its peak. Shakespeare immortalized the concept of the hot, balmy summer evening in which anything is possible, and inspired this dreamy cake.

'I know a bank whereon the wild thyme bows,
Where oxlips and the nodding violet grows
Quite over-canopied with luscious woodbine,
With sweet musk roses, and with eglantine:
There sleeps Titania some time of the night,
Lull'd in these flowers with dances and delight.'

A Midsummer Night's Dream (Act II, Scene I)

1 Prepare your Lemon Drizzle Cake tiers, covering them in pale green sugarpaste (see pages 32–35). Dowel your 20-cm/8-in. tier and stack your 15-cm/6-in. tier on top. Finish the bottom of each tier with a length of gold ribbon, secured with a little royal icing.

2 The design for this cake centres on an abundance of sugar flowers (see pages 52–53), all of which should be made in advance of the cake and ready to go. The skill in creating this cake lies in the preparatory work and should be relatively quick to assemble once the cake itself is baked. You will need to prepare around 15 each of the following: dark purple hydrangeas, brushed with a deeper purple dust colour on their edges and centre; pale yellow buttercups, brushed with yellow dust colour in their centres; violet cherry blossoms, gently pull on the bottom petal to stretch, with a white middle and dark purple eye hand painted using dusts mixed with a little alcohol; white primulas, brushed with pale yellow in their centres; white snow roses, brushed with bright pink on their petals and yellow in their centres; and a selection of leaves in deep shades of green, brushed with shades of green and brown dust colours.

3 Use a little royal icing on the back on each leaf to build up a luscious covering of leaves all around your cake. Start at the bottom and build up, allowing higher leaves to rest on lower ones, stopping as necessary to give them time to dry and firm up.

4 Begin to intersperse your foliage with blooms and blossoms, attaching each one with a little royal icing. Go for abundance. More is more. Scatter colours and shapes. Once you are happy that your cake is looking suitably covered in flowers, sprinkle with a liberal dusting of edible Hologram White glitter, which will make it sparkle like an enchanted forest.

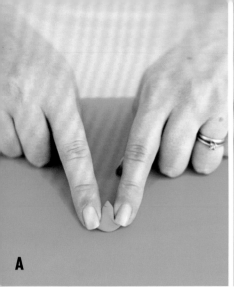

A

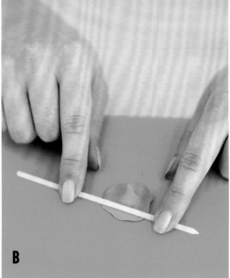

B

C

Pulled Flowers

flower paste (coloured as
    necessary using paste food
    colouring)

*light gauge florist wire, 30 g/
    1 oz. is enough for small
    flowers, prepared into 3–4
    equal-sized lengths*
*round-nose pliers or a pair of
    craft tweezers*
non-stick board
cel pin or a dowelling rod
*small blossom cutter with an
    open top (no plunger cutters)*
foam mat
*bone tool (smaller than a ball
    tool)*
edible glue
floristry tape

Pulled flowers, like hyacinths and bluebells, are made without cutters, so you will get used to working with flower paste, wires and taping sprays together – everything that constitutes a great flower maker. Plus, these make excellent filler flowers to set off the larger flowers that you will be making. The technique for making pulled flowers is known as The Mexican Hat Technique because the paste forms a sombrero-like shape.

1 Bend the very top of each wire with a pair of round nosed pliers or with craft tweezers (i.e. not the ones you do your eyebrows with!) to make a tiny hook, like a shepherd's crook. Make one wire for each flower you want to make.

2 Knead a small pinch of flower paste and roll into a ball, 1 cm/³⁄₈ in. diameter is sufficient for small blossoms. With one finger, roll gently on one half of your paste ball to create a cone shape. (**A**)

3 Sit your cone on a non-stick board with its point pointing upwards. Use your index fingers to press gently on each side of the fat bottom part of your cone so that they flatten down. Flatten all the way around the bottom, leaving the point intact. You should be starting to see the sombrero resemblance (**B**).

4 Use a cel pin or a small length of dowelling rod to roll the flattened portion of your cone out to around 1 mm/¹⁄₂₄ in. thickness. Always roll from the centre outwards.

5 Your chosen cutter should be able to slip over the top of your cone with the point sticking up through the middle. This is why you need to use open cutters for this job. We need that pointed cone section intact. Cut out your shape and wrap up any excess paste to use later. (**C**)

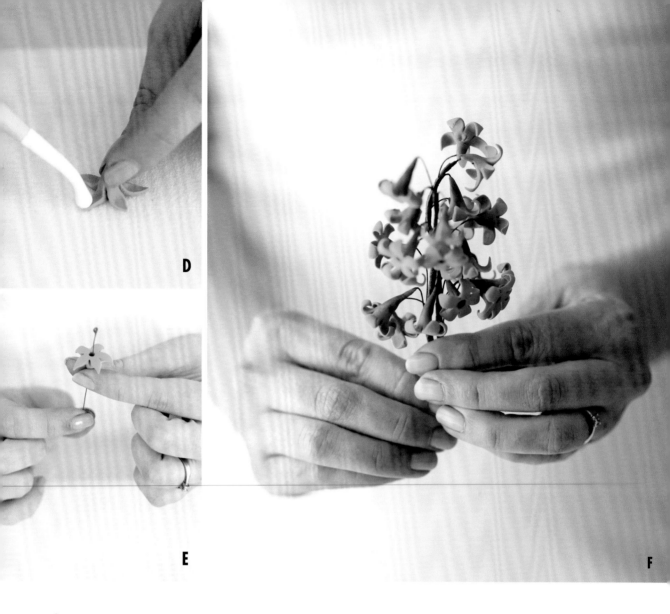

D

E

F

6 Transfer your flower shape, with its long cone section, to a foam mat and frill the edges as necessary (**D**). To make a hyacinth or a bluebell, run your ball tool along each petal down its centre from the middle of the flower to the tip of the petal.

7 Hold your flower gently and push your cel pin (or a cocktail stick/toothpick) a tiny bit into the centre of the flower head. This creates a natural looking throat.

8 Dip the hook of your wire into edible glue, wipe away any excess and carefully push the bottom of the wire into the throat of the flower until it comes out of the pointed end of your cone. From this point, you need to slowly pull the wire from the bottom (**E**) until the hook catches in the centre of the flower and can no longer be seen from the top. Pinch the point of your cone in-between your thumb and forefinger, rolling lightly to seal the neck of your flower.

9 Leave your flowers to dry overnight and then tape each wire with floristry tape. To create a spray of flowers, bind the individual wires together along one longer central wire, taping from at least 1 cm/ $^3/_8$ in. down from each flower head so that they can be bent and arranged into position (**F**).

Zombie Pin-up Cake for Halloween

20-cm/8-in. Red Velvet Cake
(see page 16), filled and
crumb-coated (see pages
26–29) with Cream Cheese
Frosting (see page 21)

1.5 kg/3⅓ lbs sugarpaste
coloured pale green (I've
used Sugarflair Spruce
Green food colouring)

250 g/9 oz. white sugarpaste

1 teaspoon CMC powder

50 g/1½ oz. red sugarpaste

edible glaze

100 g/3½ oz. sugarpaste
coloured grey

black food colouring

250 g/1⅓ cups royal icing,
coloured dark green

25-cm/10-in. cake drum/circle
green ribbon
cocktail stick/toothpick
small paintbrush
parchment piping bag fitted with
a medium open star
nozzle/tip

Serves up to 20

This cake is the perfect centrepiece to any Halloween party table. It's creepy and it's kooky but it's all together delicious. The design is completely customisable, as you will see from the nails of my zombie hand, so take my method and my tricks to create your very own spooky treat... or else I'll come and get you. Boo!

1 Prepare your Red Velvet Cake, filling and crumb-coating it with Cream Cheese Frosting, before covering in pale green sugarpaste. I favour Spruce Green for this job as it has a slightly mossy tone to it. Cover a 25-cm/10-in. cake drum/circle in the same green sugarpaste and secure your cake centrally with a little royal icing. Fix a green ribbon around the cake drum/circle to finish it off.

2 Knead the CMC powder into the white sugarpaste before adding just a little Spruce Green food colouring to create an eerie shade of off-white green, suitable for a zombie's skin tone.

3 This is where you will need to get creative. Roll 5 finger-sized pieces of sugarpaste to match the shapes and sizes of the fingers on your right hand and thumb. Pay extra attention to the wrinkles of skin where your fingers bend and scratch these onto your sugarpaste fingers with a cocktail stick/toothpick to bring them to life.

4 If your zombie is something of a deceased pin-up girl, like mine, you may want to add a glamorous touch to her fingernails. Roll little sausages of red sugarpaste (pre-coloured) and flatten them down into almond shapes to fit on the end of each of your sugarpaste fingers. Secure each nail to its finger using a dab of water. I have brushed each of my sugarpaste fingernails with edible glaze to make them shine – because I love a high gloss manicure.

5 Make your own right hand into a claw shape and arrange your sugarpaste fingers into a position to match, bending them as necessary, on top of your cake. Once you are happy with the arrangement, use a small knife to cut into the sugarpaste on top of your cake and push each finger in so they appear to be bursting out of the cake itself. Do not worry if your get a few cake crumbs coming out too, this will add to the effect and is why I think Red Velvet works best for this design.

6 Roll out your grey sugarpaste to around 3 mm/⅛ in. thick and cut small tombstone shapes from this using a sharp knife. It is more fun if the tombstones are uneven and mismatched so go freestyle on this one! Use black food colouring and a tiny paintbrush to write names on your tombstones if you are feeling gruesome! Arrange your tombstones around the bottom of your cake, securing them with the green royal icing, and pipe overgrown grass around the bottom and a little on the top of your cake. Enjoy scaring your friends with your deliciously deadly hand cake!

Candy Cane Cake for Christmas

20-cm/8-in. Classic Victoria Sponge Cake (see page 14) filled with Basic Buttercream (see page 20) and raspberry jam, crumb-coated (see pages 26–29) with Basic Buttercream (see page 20)

1.5 kg/3¼ lbs white sugarpaste

250 g/1⅓ cups royal icing, one-third of it coloured red (I've used Red Extra food colouring)

25-cm/10-in. cake drum/circle
marzipan spacers
red ribbon (15 mm/½ in. width)
double-sided tape
2 parchment piping bags each with small round piping nozzle/tip
parchment or plastic piping bag with a large open star nozzle/tip
3 red Wired Roses (see pages 72–73)

Serves up to 20

Sometimes you want to be festive without dragging out last year's Santa and plastic Rudolph. The cake is the answer – understated seasonal glamour. Have yourself a merry little Christmas, sweetie!

1 Prepare and cover the Classic Victoria Sponge Cake with 1 kg/2¼ lbs of white sugarpaste.

2 Cover your cake drum/circle with 500 g/1 lb. white sugarpaste by rolling out to the thickness of your marzipan spacers, brushing a little water on the drum/circle and then laying the sugarpaste on top. Smooth your sugarpaste down using a straight-edge smoother and then trim the excess away as if you were trimming a pie dish – hold the drum at eye-level from underneath and run a large sharp knife all around the edges of the drum until the excess falls away. Finish the edges of your cake drum/circle with red ribbon, secured with double-sided tape.

3 Mix up your royal icing, colouring half of it scarlet red using Red Extra food colouring (or a similarly bright red). Fill 2 parchment piping bags, both fitted with small round piping nozzles/tips, with your 2 royal icing colours. Pipe a little white royal icing on the middle of your covered cake drum/circle and carefully place your cake centrally on the drum/circle.

4 To create the candy cane stripes around the side of your cake, begin with your white royal icing and small round nozzle/tip and pipe gently until the icing connects with the top edge of your cake. Continue squeezing the piping bag and pull your nozzle 5 cm/2 in. or so away from the cake and gently downwards. An unbroken line of icing should be coming from your nozzle and the pull of gravity should be guiding it down in a perfectly vertical line. When you have nearly reached the bottom of your cake, stop squeezing and continue to guide your piping nozzle/tip down to connect with the bottom edge before pulling away. I am not going to lie; this takes practice so start with the white icing!

5 Carry on piping white pinstripes all around the sides of your cake at regular intervals before repeating this process with the red royal icing to create red pinstripes between white ones.

6 Use a piping bag fitted with a large open star nozzle/tip to pipe a shell border along the top and bottom edges of your cake. This will conceal the points at which your pinstripes start and finish for a more seamless appearance. To pipe your shells, hold your nozzle at a 45° angle and squeeze gently until you are happy with the size of your shell. Stop squeezing and pull your piping bag around the cake until the shell tails off. Repeat this step this time piping over the tail of your last shell to create the illusion of a line of perfect shells.

7 Crown your cake with 3 beautiful red Wired Roses and a few rose leaves. Place a small ball of leftover white sugarpaste at the centre of your cake and gently push the stems of your roses into it to hold them securely. Leave your cake to dry for a few hours before serving up with festive cheer.

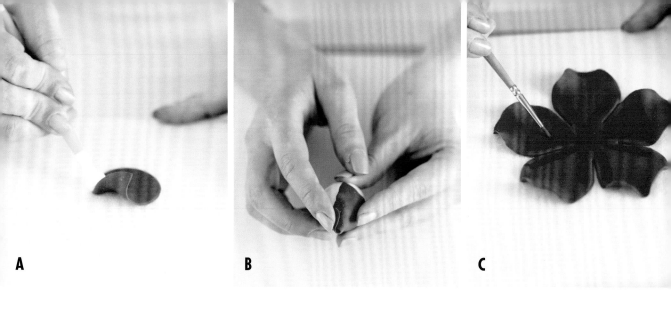

A   **B**   **C**

Wired Roses

150 g/5 oz. flower paste

28-mm/1-in. cel bud
cocktail stick/toothpick
20-gauge floristry wire
  green/white
non-stick board
small non-stick rolling pin
5-petal easy rose cutter
  (15 mm/¹⁄₂ in.)
foam mat
ball tool
edible glue
small paintbrush
green flower paste
calyx cutter
green floristry tape

1 Begin by preparing your cel bud to be the centre of your rose. You should see a line running around the centre of the bud – push a cocktail stick/toothpick horizontally through the bud at the same level as this line. This creates a tunnel for you to push your wire through. Use a whole length of wire and, with your bud at the centre of the wire, pull both ends down and twist them into one double-strength wire.

2 Knead and roll out enough flowerpaste to cut a single petal of 2 mm/¹⁄₁₆ in. thickness using your 5-petal cutter, trimming as necessary with a sharp knife. Transfer this petal to your foam mat and with your ball tool pressed half on the edge of your petal and half on the mat, drag the ball firmly around the petal (**A**). You should notice that the edges start to 'frill', meaning they become thinner and appear to have movement.

3 Paint the top half of your wired cel bud with a little edible glue and wrap your first petal around it . Lay your petal horizontally with its point facing left, wrapping the petal clockwise so that the point is underneath the rest of your petal. Look from the top and check that you have created a tight coil and that you cannot see the white polystyrene of your bud. (**B**)

4 To create your first layer of petals, knead and roll out enough flower paste to cut out the full shape from your 5-petal cutter at around 2 mm/¹⁄₁₆ in. thickness. Tap the back of your cutter to remove the shape (you may need to encourage it out with a cocktail stick/toothpick) and transfer to your foam mat. Frill the edges of each petal with your ball tool pressed half on and half off as you did in step 2.

5 Paint a little edible glue in the middle of your 5-petals and up the sides of each individual petal. For this layer only, you will also need to glue inside two of the petals going half way up each one. The best way to remember which ones to glue is to look at your 5-petals with one petal at the top – this is the head. The shape now has a head, two arms, and two legs – glue the two arms. (**C**)

6 Shake the 5-petals into your hand and carefully push the wire of your bud down through the middle of the petals. Wrap the first glued arm piece around the bud, followed by the second arm directly opposite. That was another full layer. Glue your last three petals around evenly spaced and each overlapping the last until you have another full layer. (**D**)

D

E

F

7 For your next layer, repeat step 4, but this time you will need to curl the outer edges of each petal around a cocktail stick/toothpick to create the illusion of the petals unfurling from the rose (**E**). Turn the petals over so that the curled edges are facing downwards and glue half way up the edges of each petal with a little dab in the centre. Shake this into your hand and push the wire through the centre, bringing each petal up to the rose in turn, the next overlapping the last until you have completed another full layer of petals around the rose. Leave this layer to dry before moving on. (**F**)

8 Repeat step 7 until you are happy with the size of your rose. It is not uncommon to repeat this stage up to five times for a full flower. You may need to hang your rose upside down to dry each layer for 30 minutes once the rose starts getting big. Finish your rose with a calyx – this should be made from green flower paste, rolled to 2 mm/^{1}/$_{16}$ in. thickness and cut out using a 5-cm/2-in. calyx cutter. Frill the edges of this gently on your foam mat and attach with a little edible glue. (**G**) Trim your wire to the length you need it to be and wrap with green floristry wire to create a stem. You can wrap tissue paper around your wire before you bind to create a thicker stem (**H**).

G

H

Effortlessly Elegant

Filigree Rose Cupcakes

12 cupcakes in the flavour of
your choice (see pages
14–18), baked in silver
foil cases

500 g/1 lb. sugarpaste,
coloured pale grey (I've
used Liquorice paste food
colouring)

silver edible lustre spray

125 g/⅔ cup white
royal icing

12 white sugarpaste roses (see
pages 78–79, but use plain
white sugarpaste)

*parchment piping bag fitted with
a small round nozzle/tip*

Makes 12

The inspiration for this simple design came from a publicity shot of Mae West, which I was, funnily enough, studying for retro hair ideas. As I find myself wandering through a world of pastel pink and cutesy rustic cupcakes, there is something in the glamour of a monochromatic colour scheme that appeals to me. I think these scream 1930s old Hollywood glamour and I hope you'll agree.

1 Cover your cupcakes with pale grey sugarpaste (see pages 30–31). Don't forget to include a cheeky buttercream surprise in each one!

2 If you want to add a little extra sparkle to your cupcakes, spray the top of each one with silver edible lustre spray (these spray cans are easily found in most large supermarkets and craft stores) and allow to dry before moving on.

3 Fill your piping bag (see pages 38–39) with white royal icing and, using a small round nozzle/tip, pipe swirling lines that interconnect and sprawl over the top of your cupcake. If you look at my own design, you will see that the lines are all piped freehand with no real rhyme or reason, so this is a great design to try your hand at if you are new to royal icing.

4 Pipe a small dot of royal icing onto the centre of your cupcakes and gently press a white sugarpaste rose proudly atop each one. You can make your sugarpaste roses up to 1–2 weeks in advance of decorating these cupcakes, using the technique shown on pages 77–78.

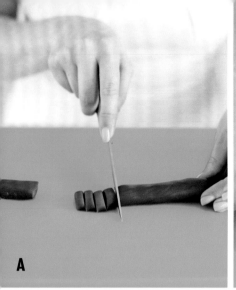

A

B

C

Sugarpaste Roses

150 g/5 oz. sugarpaste for 12 roses (you can use sugarpaste with added CMC if you want your roses to hold a little stiffer)

plastic document wallet
small knife

One of the very first flowers that you should learn to make is the sugarpaste rose. The equipment required to make these is minimal and, with practice, you will find that you can produce large quantities of these roses at a fair pace! Sugarpaste roses can be made up to 1–2 weeks in advance if stored in a cardboard box in a cool, dry place.

1 Begin by kneading your sugarpaste to warm it up (see page 35). I have used pre-coloured sugarpaste for these roses, as I wanted a fairly deep red colour. Start with white when you are learning as this is by far the least messy option!

2 Roll your sugarpaste into a sausage shape of around 2 cm/$^3/_4$ in. thickness and cut 6 fat discs 5 mm/$^1/_4$ in. thick using a knife. (**A**)

3 Lay your sugarpaste discs inside the plastic document wallet, close the wallet and press down gently on top of each disc with your thumb to flatten. You do not need them to be paper thin, just a little bit flatter. (**B**)

4 Run a fingertip along the top edge of each disc to flatten it further (**C**). You do not need to go all around the disc as we want the top edge to be thinner than the bottom edge. As you form your rose, remember to keep these thin edges as the top edge of what should now look like petals.

D

E

F

5 Open up your plastic wallet and carefully peel off your smallest disc, rolling it around into a tight coil with the thin edge at the top. This one petal now forms the centre of your rose. (**D**)

6 Lay another 2 petals evenly around the first to form a second layer of petals. I find it easiest to wrap the second petal around the first and to position the third petal opposite the second. The sugarpaste will adhere to itself. (**E**)

7 Your remaining 3 petals will make up the third layer of your rose. Wrap these around so that they are evenly spaced. (**F**)

8 You can now trim the excess sugarpaste away from the bottom of your rose and gently pinch the edges of your outer petals to add movement. (**G**)

9 Your beautiful sugarpaste rose is now ready (**H**). If you would like to create a larger rose, you can always add a fourth layer of petals made up of a further 4 petals. Add these in exactly the same way as before, wrapping each petal around so that the 4 are evenly spaced around your rose.

G

H

White Rose Romance

20-cm/8-in. and 15-cm/6-in. Lemon Drizzle Cake tiers (see page 15)

2 kg/4⅓ lbs white sugarpaste, plus extra to hold the wires for the sugar flowers

250 g/1⅓ cups royal icing

1 white Wired Rose (see pages 72–73)

25-cm/10-in. cake drum/circle
marzipan spacers
white ribbon
double-sided tape
4 dowelling rods
parchment piping bag fitted with a large open star nozzle/tip
parchment piping bag fitted with a large leaf nozzle/tip

Serves up to 34

The white rose is the epitome of elegance. For me, they come loaded with thoughts of my Yorkist mother and her love of medieval English history (look it up, kids), as well as happy memories of the bouquets I surprised my bridesmaids with on my wedding day. White roses are a blank canvas upon which you can paint your own romantic story.

1 Begin by preparing your Lemon Drizzle Cake tiers and covering both in white sugarpaste (see pages 32–35).

2 Cover your 25-cm/10-in. cake drum/circle with 500 g/1 lb 2 oz. white sugarpaste by rolling it out to the thickness of your marzipan spacers, brushing a little water on the drum/circle and then laying the sugarpaste on top. Smooth your sugarpaste down using a straight-edge smoother and then trim the excess away as if you were trimming a pie dish. Smooth any rough edges by gently running your finger around the edge of the drum. Finish the edges of your cake drum/circle with white ribbon, secured with double-sided tape.

3 Fix the 20-cm/8-in. tier to your cake drum/circle with a little royal icing. Dowel your 20 cm/8 in. tier and stack your 15-cm/6-in. tier on top (see pages 36–37).

4 Using a piping bag fitted with a large open star nozzle/tip to pipe a shell border along the bottom edges of your tiers. To pipe your shells, hold your nozzle/tip at a 45° angle and squeeze gently until you are happy with the size of your shell. Stop squeezing and pull your piping bag around the cake until the shell tails off. Repeat this step this time piping over the tail of your last shell so that this appears as one unbroken line.

5 Use a piping bag fitted with a large leaf nozzle/tip to pipe a ruffle trim along the top edges of your tiers. You will need to angle your piping bag so that the opening of the leaf nozzle/tip is horizontal and squeeze gently until the icing makes contact with the cake. As you continue to squeeze gently and move around the top edge of your cake, you will need to rock your piping nozzle/tip back and forth so that the line of icing folds over itself. Practice a little on your work surface if you need to, but any mistakes can be easily wiped away when working with white on white.

6 Top your cake with a white Wired Rose.

Mother of Pearl Cookies

250 g/9 oz. royal icing
12 Basic Cookies (see page
   19), cut using a 5-cm/2-in.
   round cookie cutter
250 g/9 oz. white sugarpaste
   with 1 teaspoon CMC
   kneaded in
pearlescent white metallic food
   paint
pearlescent shimmer dust
white sugar flowers
   (see pages 52–53)
pearl dragees

*parchment piping bag fitted with
   a small round nozzle/tip
cocktail stick/toothpick
squeezy plastic bottle
flower cutter and matching
   moulds (I have used Snow
   Rose, Petunia and
   Hydrangea)
small non-stick rolling pin
flat paintbrush*

Makes 12

These cookies would look more at home in your jewellery box than in your cookie jar! Deceptively quick and easy to make – especially if you make the sugar flowers ahead of time – these little treats are certain to delight and add a touch of elegance to any cup of tea.

1 Mix up your royal icing until it holds stiff peaks before spooning 2–3 tablespoons into a parchment piping bag fitted with a small round nozzle/tip (see pages 38–39). Ensure that any icing you are not using is covered with clingfilm/plastic wrap to prevent it from drying out.

2 Pipe a line of icing around the top edge of each cookie. This technique of icing cookies is known as 'flooding' so you are, in effect, piping a 'floodgate' that will contain the icing neatly on top of your cookie. Insert a cocktail stick/toothpick into the piping nozzle/tip to act as a stopper and set the bag aside to be used later.

3 Add sufficient cold water to your remaining royal icing to change the consistency from stiff icing to 'seven-second' icing. You are aiming for a runny consistency where a spoon removed from stirring the icing will leave a ripple that disappears in the count of seven, leaving a perfectly flat surface. Pour this icing into a squeezy plastic bottle.

4 Squeeze your runny icing on top of your cookies, filling up the cookie but leaving a 5 mm/$\frac{1}{4}$ in. gap from the floodgate line of icing so that your runny icing has space to settle into. Gently tease your runny icing to the floodgate line using a cocktail stick/toothpick. Leave your cookies to dry for 1 hour to avoid damaging the surface as you decorate.

5 Finish your cookies by encrusting them with white sugar flowers made using your cutter and mould sets (see pages 52–53). Allow your flowers to dry before dusting them with a pearlescent shimmer dust and sticking a pearl dragee into the centre of each one with a small blob of royal icing. Stick your flowers around the edges of your cookies with a little royal icing and scatter a few more pearl dragees into the centre of each cookie.

Polka Pearl Cake

20-cm/8-in. Red Velvet Cake (see page 16) covered with 1 kg/2¼ lbs white sugarpaste (see pages 32–35), plus extra to hold the wires for the sugar flowers

125 g/⅔ cup royal icing

pearlescent white metallic food paint

3 white Sugar Peonies (see pages 46–47)

6 stems of Sugar Lily of the Valley (see pages 86–87)

white ribbon

parchment piping bag fitted with a medium round piping nozzle/tip

paintbrush

Serves up to 20

I find myself wearing pearls most days. My jewellery box is awash with necklaces in various sizes, earrings and bracelets. There is something just so glamorous about pearls and they make the very same impact on cakes as they do against skin.

1 Prepare your Red Velvet Cake and cover with white sugarpaste. It's best to leave this overnight to set before decorating if you can to avoid damaging the finish while working. Secure a simple white ribbon around the bottom of your cake with a little royal icing at the back.

2 Fill a parchment piping bag fitted with a medium piping nozzle/tip with white royal icing and pipe a series of large 1 cm/³⁄₈ in. dots at regular intervals around the bottom of your cake, around 1 cm/³⁄₈ in. above your ribbon. Use your ribbon as a guide to keep your line of pearls straight. You may find it easier to pipe one pearl and then turn the cake to pipe directly opposite on the other side. As a cheeky cheat, you will find that some professional cake decorating turntables have points marked at regular intervals, which you can follow.

3 Pipe a second line of dots around the top edge of your cake, directly above your bottom line of dots. Repeat this with a middle line of dots around the middle of your cake, with each dot sitting in the middle of your top and bottom lines.

4 Allow the pearls to dry for at least 3 hours before painting with Pearlescent White metallic food paint to bring them to life.

5 Crown your cake with an arrangement of white Sugar Peonies and Sugar Lily of the Valley. Place a golf ball-sized ball of left-over white sugarpaste at the middle of your cake and use this to push your flower wires into to hold your arrangement securely.

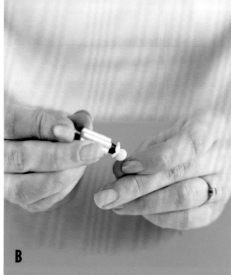

A

B

C

Sugar Lily of the Valley

This is a beautiful bloom that never fails to bring back happy memories of my Nana. I often recall the scent of soap in her bathroom as I craft these tiny blossoms and am so pleased that this oh so English flower has found its way back into the bridal bouquet – and onto the wedding cake as a result!

white flower paste

green flower paste

2 tablespoons pale yellow royal icing (in a piping bag with a small round nozzle/tip)

non-stick board

small non-stick rolling pin

30-gauge green floristry wire —(cut into quater lengths)

edible glue

tiny blossom plunger cutter

26-gauge green or white floristry wire (cut into third lengths)

green floristry tape

veined cel board

small knife

green dust colour

1 Work a small amount of white flower paste between your fingers to warm it before rolling into a pea-sized ball.

2 Make a small hook in the end of each of your 30-gauge wires. You will need 12 wires per stem of blossoms. Dip the hook of one of your wires into edible glue and then pull the wire through each ball of flower paste until the hook is caught and concealed in its centre (**A**). Reshape your ball of paste as necessary and put aside to dry. I find it helpful to stand my wires in a polystyrene block or cake dummy.

3 Repeat this process for all 12 of your wires, as many times over as you require to make your stems. These balls will form both the unopened buds of your flower and the base of the opened flowers too.

4 Use a tiny blossom plunger cutter (see page 52) to cut blossoms from rolled-out flower paste (**B**). You should aim to roll your paste to around 2-mm/^{1}/$_{16}$-in. thick. Dab a little edible glue on the top of one of your wired balls and plunge the blossom shape directly onto it. The plunger should create a centre in the middle of your blossom, making it look like it is opening. For each stem, make 7 of these flowering heads and leave 5 wired balls as unopened buds. Leave these to dry completely for at least 1 hour.

5 To wire your Sugar Lily of the Valley stems, take a length of 26-gauge wire as your base and wire your 5 buds, one at a time, each slightly lower than the last. Use green floristry tape to attach each wire, pulling the tape taut and wrapping it around the wires to bind the thinner wire of your bud to the thicker central wire of the stem. Once you have attached all 5 buds, continue this same process for your 7 flowering heads. (**C**)

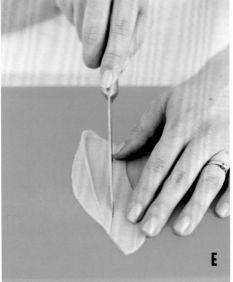

6 Finish your flowers by piping a tiny yellow dot of royal icing into the centre of each flowering head. Make sure that you leave these to dry overnight before arranging them on a cake to avoid damaging these tiny centres. (**D**)

7 To make a leaf to wrap around the flower stem, roll out a small amount of green flower paste on a veined cel board. Cut a freehand leaf shape, long enough to run alongside your flowers, with a small knife, ensuring that the vein of the leaf is running straight along its centre. (**E**)

8 Dip a length of 30-gauge green floristry wire into edible glue and carefully insert this into the vein of your leaf (**F**). Stop when the wire is half the way up the vein and lay the leaf to dry for a few hours until completely dry.

9 Brush the leaf with green dust colour (**G**) to add depth and shade. Tape the wire of the leaf to a stem of flowers and arrange as required. (**H**)

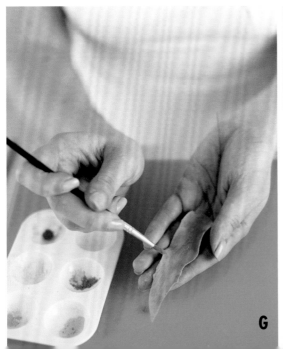

Glamorous Ganache Cake

20-cm/8-in. Chocolate Mud
Cake (see page 17), filled
with Chocolate Buttercream
(see page 20) and crumb-
coated (see pages 26–29)
with Basic Buttercream
(see page 20)

White Chocolate Ganache
(see page 22)

100 g/3½ oz. white modelling
chocolate mixed with ½
teaspoon CMC powder

icing/confectioners' sugar

Hologram white edible glitter

gold dragees

20-cm/8-in. cake drum/circle
25-cm/10-in. cake drum/circle
double-sided tape
cheeky leopard print ribbon
plastic piping bag fitted with a
*   small round piping nozzle/tip*
small non-stick rolling pin
flower cutters and matching
*   moulds*

Serves up to 20

Ganache-covered cakes can be glamorous too! I hope that this design will inspire you to take a few of the techniques that we regularly use for sugarpaste covered cakes and drag them kicking and screaming into chocolate. I had heard tales of folk who do not like sugarpaste icing so this would be a great alternative for them. Oddballs.

1 Prepare your Chocolate Mud Cake and refrigerate it for 30 minutes to set.

2 Fix your 20-cm/8-in. cake on a 20-cm/8-in. cake drum/circle, set on a larger 25-cm/10-in. cake drum/circle using a little double-sided tape.

3 Cover your cake in a smooth layer of White Chocolate Ganache, using the crumb-coating technique on pages 26–29. Try to get the finish as smooth as you can but do not worry if there are any slight imperfections as we will easily cover these with decoration.

4 Spread White Chocolate Ganache over the silver of the 25 cm/10 in. cake drum/circle and wrap a fabulous leopard print ribbon around it.

5 Fill a plastic piping bag, fitted with a small round piping nozzle/tip, with more of your White Chocolate Ganache. Plastic piping bags are preferable for this task as they are sturdier than parchment. Use this piping bag to pipe interconnecting swirls of filigree around the top edges of your cake. You can choose to go freehand with this design, but try to bring your filigree lines down onto the sides of your cake at regular intervals. I have worked my design down at 4 equal points around my cake.

6 To make your white chocolate flowers, roll out some white chocolate modelling paste on a surface lightly dusted with icing/confectioners' sugar. You will need your chocolate to be around 2-mm/$^1/_{16}$-in. thick. Cut out your flowers and shape them in their matching moulds. Leave these flowers to dry on a bumpy surface made of crumpled baking parchment so that they will hold their shape. A liberal sprinkling of edible glitter will make these babies dazzle.

7 Fix your chocolate flowers to your cake using a little ganache as glue. Pipe a dot of ganache into the centre of each flower and gently press a gold dragee inside. Gold dragees can be scattered around the surface of your cake, pressed gently into the surface of the ganache.

8 Finish your design by piping a line of dots around the bottom edge of your cake. The quickest way to do this is to squeeze your piping bag until you are happy with the size of the dot, stop squeezing and drag your nozzle/tip around to the centre point of where you want your next dot to be. Squeeze your piping bag again until the next dot of icing is the same size as the first and covers the line where you dragged your piping bag. You should be left with a line of dots that nuzzle up to each other nicely. Serve to your family and friends and sit back as the compliments flood your way.

Jet & Lace Cake

20-cm/8-in. Salted Caramel
Cake (see page 18), crumb-
coated (see page 26–29) in
Salted Caramel Buttercream
(see page 20) and covered
in Nude sugarpaste (see
pages 32–35), coloured
using Peach paste food
colouring

125 g/²⁄₃ cup royal icing,
coloured black (I've used
Black Extra paste food
colouring)

black Wired Rose (see pages
72–73)

*66 x 10-cm/26 x 4-in. baking
parchment collar, trimmed to
fit the cake perfectly*
*scribe tool or cocktail stick/
toothpick*
*parchment piping bag fitted with
a small round piping
nozzle/tip*
black lace ribbon

Serves up to 20

I adore the elegance of a monochrome cake. A simple nude-coloured cake
provides the perfect contrast for a handpiped design in black and shows up
the delicate detailing of your black lace.

1 Begin by preparing your Salted Caramel Cake, crumb-coating it in Salted Caramel Buttercream and
then covering it in Nude sugarpaste. Allow your sugarpaste to dry on your cake overnight if possible
before decorating to avoid damaging the surface while decorating.

2 Wrap a length of baking parchment around the sides of your cake and trim to fit. Fold this length
into 8 equal sections. Use a glass, cup or small plate to draw a semi-circle onto the top edge of your
folded parchment. Aim to make this semi-circle approximately 2.5 cm/1 in. from the top of your paper
at its lowest point. Cut along the line that you have drawn and open up your parchment to reveal a
collar with 8 equal swags cut into it.

3 Wrap the parchment collar around your cake, securing with a little tape, and carefully score along
the swag lines with a scribe tool or cocktail stick/toothpick.

4 Remove and refold your collar and repeat step 3 to create a second semi-circle line below your first.
Once you are happy with the position of this second swag line, cut along the line and repeat step 4.

5 Fill a parchment piping bag, fitted with a small round piping nozzle/tip, with black royal icing.
The only way that you will achieve this depth of black (starting from white icing!) is by using an extra
concentrated black food colouring paste such as Black Extra.

6 Hold your piping bag very close to but not touching the surface of your cake and pipe small dots
along the swag lines that you've made. You will find it easier to start with the top line all the way
around your cake, following this with the lower line. Pipe a vertical line of 3 dots at the highest point of
each swag. Finish your hand-piped design with a teardrop at the bottom of each vertical line of dots. Create
your teardrop by piping a fourth dot a little lower than your vertical line of 3, dragging your piping nozzle/
tip upwards instead of pulling directly away when you are happy with the size of the dot your have piped.

7 Wrap a length of black lace ribbon around the bottom edge of your cake, securing at the back with a
little black royal icing.

8 Top your cake with a single black wired rose. I think it looks fabulous to tie a bow around the stem
of this rose in the same black lace that you used around the bottom of the cake.

Organic Lines Ombré Cake

20-cm/8-in. and 15-cm/6-in.
Classic Victoria Sponge Cake
tiers (see page 14) filled
with Cream Cheese
Frosting (see page 21) or
Buttercream (see page 20)
and raspberry jam
selection of whole fruits – such
as cherries, strawberries
and blueberries
1 UK large, US extra large
egg white
caster/superfine sugar
Cream Cheese Frosting
(see page 21)
Dusky Pink paste food
colouring

4 dowelling rods
20-cm/8-in. and 25-cm/10-in.
cake drums/circles
double-sided sticky tape
icing turntable
large palette knife
side scraper
dusky pink ribbon

Serves up to 34

Ombré! Undeniably the buzzword of the last few years, this design is a very easy way of bringing a little ombré to your table in impressive fashion.

1 Begin by preparing your 20-cm/8-in. and 15-cm/6-in. Classic Victoria Sponge Cake tiers, filling them with raspberry jam and a little Cream Cheese Frosting or Buttercream. Set your 20-cm/8-in. cake onto a 20-cm/8-in. cake drum/circle.

2 Fix your 20-cm/8-in. tier to a larger 25-cm/10-in. cake drum/circle. A cross of double-sided tape in the centre of your 25-cm/10-in. cake drum should be sufficient to stick the 2 tiers together.

3 Prepare the sugared fruits, which will be the finishing touch to your beautiful cake. To sugar a fruit is a quick and simple task of painting with a thin layer of egg white before immediately sprinkling with or dipping into caster/superfine sugar. Sugared fruits should be allowed to dry for 2–3 hours before being arranged on your cake.

4 Crumb-coat your tiers with Cream Cheese Frosting using the same technique as shown on pages 26–29. Allow the tiers to set for 30 minutes in the fridge.

5 Divide your remaining Cream Cheese Frosting evenly between 2 bowls and colour 1 bowl with Dusky Pink paste food colouring.

6 Remove your 15-cm/6-in. tier from the fridge and spread a thick layer of white Cream Cheese Frosting over the top and half way down the sides of the cake. Spoon a little of your pink Cream Cheese Frosting into your white and combine into a shade of pale pink and spread this thickly around the bottom half of your 15-cm/6-in. tier.

7 Clean off your large palette knife and hold the tip of the blade so that it is gently pressed against the top edge of the side of your cake. Without moving the blade, slowly turn your turntable anticlockwise (assuming that you are holding the knife in your right hand and turning with your left) so that you are creating a line in the frosting. As you reach one full rotation, gently move your blade down to create a second line directly under your first. As you continue to move around the cake, bring the blade downwards in this same way until you reach the bottom. The cake should have a pattern of organic lines that have blended the 2 shades of frosting into each other.

8 Tidy up the top edges of your 15-cm/6-in. tier using your side scraper, pulling all top edges into the centre of the cake.

9 Repeat step 6 with your 20-cm/8-in. tier, this time using your pink Cream Cheese Frosting on the top and half way down the sides, before pausing to add a little more Dusky Pink paste food colouring to your remaining pink frosting. Spread this darker shade of pink around the bottom half of your 20-cm/8-in. tier.

10 Repeat step 7 with your 20-cm/8-in. tier, being careful to ensure that the dowelling rods are still exposed and still slightly higher than the top of your frosted cake.

11 Spread a little dark pink frosting around the bottom of your cake to cover the silver of your 20-cm/8-in. cake drum/circle and finish the edges of this drum with a pink ribbon. Carefully stack your 15-cm/6-in. tier on top of the 20-cm/8 in. tier. Finish the cake with the sugared fruits, which you'd prepared in advance.

Falling Magnolia Cake

Sugar Magnolias (see pages 100–101)

20-cm/8-in. Lemon Drizzle Cake (see page 15), filled with lemon curd and buttercream

1 quantity Buttercream (see page 20), minus the amount used to fill the Lemon Drizzle Cake, coloured using a scant amount of Dusky Pink paste food colouring

Hot pink dust colour

plastic piping bag fitted with a large open star piping nozzle/tip
plastic posy pick

Serves up to 20

I want to show you once more how simple buttercreamed cakes can be elegant enough to take centre stage at any celebration. This design makes stars of our sugar Magnolias which can be made weeks or even months in advance, making this design something very quick to produce.

1 You can make your Sugar Magnolias up to 1 month in advance of preparing this cake (see pages 100–101). I have made 6 flowers and dusted their edges using hot pink dust colour. The flowers have been wired together into two separate branches of 3 flowers.

2 Prepare your Lemon Drizzle Cake by filling with a layer of lemon curd and buttercream. Colour your remaining buttercream to a pale shade of rose-white using a tiny amount of Dusky Pink paste food colouring. Crumb-coat your cake with the pale pink buttercream (see pages 26–29) and refrigerate for 1 hour.

3 I have placed my cake directly onto its serving plate but you could fix your cake to a 25-cm/10-in. cake drum/circle using a little double-sided tape. If you do this, you will need to spread pale pink buttercream over the silver of the cake drum/circle and wrap a ribbon around its edge to finish it off.

4 Fill a plastic piping bag, fitted with a large open star nozzle/tip, with pale pink buttercream and pipe a shell border around the bottom of your cake. To pipe your shells, hold your nozzle at a 45° angle and squeeze gently until you are happy with the size of your shell. Stop squeezing and pull your piping bag around the cake until the shell tails off. Repeat this step this time piping over the tail of your last shell so that this appears as one unbroken line.

5 Insert the plastic posy pick into the top of your cake so that only the very top edge is still exposed and use this to hold the bottom end of one Magnolia branch. It helps to first do this without securing the branch but bending it into the shape that it will need to take to trail down the side of your cake. Once you are happy with the position, remove the branch and pipe a little royal icing into your posy pick before inserting your branch once more. When the royal icing dries, your branch will be very secure inside the posy pick, which is held securely in your cake. Alternatively, if the cake is not travelling far, you can bind the 2 branches into 1 long branch and carefully lay this across the front top edge of your cake and allow the branch to bend and trail down the front.

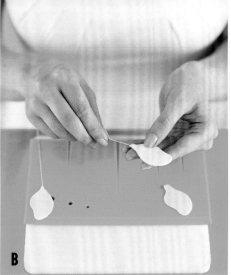

Sugar Magnolias

I love magnolias, particularly big and open and tinged with hot pink, but I only see them very rarely on a cake. So here is an easy way to top your cake with a really show-stopping bloom.

150 g/5 oz. flower paste

*4 lengths of 26-gauge white
   floristry wire (each cut into
   3 equal pieces)*
small craft scissors
cel board
small non-stick rolling pin
set of 3 magnolia petal cutters
foam mat
ball tool
edible glue
*large round fruit tray (e.g. apple,
   mango or avocado)*
brown floristry tape

1 Begin by making the bud to sit in the centre of your magnolia. Roll a ball of flower paste around 2.5 cm/ 1 inch in diameter and shape into a cone by pinching half of the ball. Create a tiny hook at the top of one of your wires and dip this in edible glue. Push the bottom of your wire through the cone so that the hook will catch inside it, stopping when the hook is in the centre.

2 Use a small knife to make ridges around the bottom half of the cone and, using a small pair of craft scissors, cut tiny little triangles into the paste around the middle (**A**). These should look a bit like the spikes on a pineapple. Keep cutting in this way so that you are creating lines of spikes, one above the other, until you reach the very top with a few snips to make the top spiky too. Leave to dry.

3 Knead and roll out sufficient white flower paste to cover 3 of the long veined sections of your cel board. Aim to get your paste nice and thin so that you can almost see through it.

4 Press your smallest magnolia petal cutter onto your paste so that one of the long veins will run down its centre. Repeat twice more to make 3 small petals.

5 Dip one of your small wires into edible glue and scrape the excess off on the side of your glue pot. Turn your petal onto its face and gently push your wire up into the vein along its back until you are around halfway up the whole petal (**B**). Gently pinch the bottom of the petal around the wire. Repeat for each petal.

6 Transfer your petals to a foam mat and, vein-side down, gently frill by running a ball tool around the edges of the petal (**C**). If you ensure that your ball tool is positioned half on the petal and half on the mat, you should get a nice movement. Leave to dry, slightly curled up at the end, in a large round fruit tray.

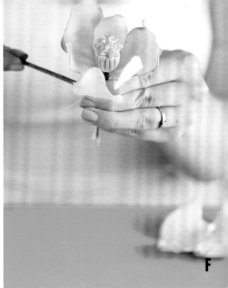

D **E** **F**

7 Repeat steps 2–5 to make 3 petals using your medium magnolia petal cutter and then another 3 with the largest one. Leave all nine of your petals to dry in the fruit tray preferably overnight (**D**).

8 Once your petals are dry you can add colour using blossom tint dusts. When making pink magnolias, I dust the whole petal with a very pale pink (just off white) and the edges with a hot pink (**E**). I then add a tiny amount of green or brown to the very bottom of each petal. When I want to make a white magnolia, I dust a scant amount of green at the bottom of each petal continuing a little way up the centre.

9 To assemble a magnolia, wrap each wire in brown floristry tape, including the bud and create 3 layers from the centre. Start by taping your 3 smallest petals to the bud so that they are evenly spaced. Repeat this with the 3 medium petals in between each small petal (**F**). Finish with your final 3 large petals cupping the smaller petals above them (**G**).

10 You can now manipulate the petals and arrange them so that you are happy with them. As a finishing touch, I always like to add a couple of green leaves to give the impression of a real magnolia. If you want to add these, see page 87 to see how to make them.

G **H**

Gloriously Opulent

Wisteria Stained Glass Cake

20-cm/8-in. Lemon Drizzle
Cake (see page 15)

blossom tint food colours (I've
used Aubergine, Navy Blue,
Petal Blue, Emerald Green
and White)

1 kg/2¼ lbs white sugarpaste

125 g/⅔ cup royal icing
(coloured black using Black
Extra food colouring paste)

artist's palette or a small plate

clear alcohol (you can use water
but alcohol dries far quicker;
vodka works best)

plastic pipette

small paintbrushes

parchment piping bag fitted with
a medium round piping
nozzle/tip

parchment piping bag fitted with
a small round piping
nozzle/tip

Serves up to 20

A stained-glass effect is relatively simple to create on a cake — all you need is inspiration, forethought and patience! My inspiration for this cake came from a Tiffany lamp with the most incredible violet and blue Wisteria design.

1 Begin by preparing your Lemon Drizzle Cake and covering it in white sugarpaste (see pages 32–35). Allow this to dry overnight before decorating to avoid damaging the surface of the icing as you work.

2 Essentially, the pattern for this cake is that of trailing branches of wisteria hanging down from the centre point of your cake. While I would not have the patience to mark each tiny area that I intend to paint before getting stuck in to this design, I do think it's prudent to scratch a few lines from the centre of your cake to denote where the branches of your wisteria will hang and where to build your colours up from. For symmetry, I have marked 6 lines from the top centre of my cake, weaving their way down to a couple of centimetres/an inch down the cake's sides.

3 Prepare your paints in an artist's palette or on a plate. A few drops of vodka, or any clear alcohol, in a pipette turns blossom tint colours into the most wonderful paints to use on icing. I have used Aubergine, Navy Blue, Petal Blue, Emerald Green and White to create 2 shades of purple, a dark blue, a light blue and a good leafy green. If you find that your paints dry out as you work, bring them back to life with a drop of vodka.

4 Build up your design, starting with splashes of green at the top of your cake for the leaves of your wisteria, interspersed with flashes of light blue. You may find your sanity stays more intact if you work on one of your 6 marked branches at a time. Start with those leaves and then build up vines of purples and blues, working down your cake and stopping just short of the bottom.

5 Repeat step 4 until each of your 6 branches has been filled, using any space between your trailing wisteria blooms to paint in more leaves and patches of light blue. Leave the cake to dry for 30 minutes.

6 Spoon 3–4 tablespoons of your black royal icing into a parchment piping bag fitted with a medium round nozzle. Starting at the top centre of your cake, pipe thick branches along your 6 marked branch lines. These may be tricky to see by now but just aim your branches to meander down from the centre of the cake to the beginnings of your purple wisteria blooms. To make these branches look more organic, pipe a few small branches coming off of each main branch. Pipe a large flat black dot in the centre of your cake to contain your 6 branches.

7 Fill a second parchment piping bag, fitted with a small round nozzle/tip, with black royal icing and use this to carefully outline small sections of colour. If you are working to emulate a stained glass design of your own, you will find it much easier to work with the picture in front of you as a reference. By all means, use this picture as your own reference point and repeat the design around your own cake.

8 Once you have completed this design, mount your cake on a beautiful stand and set in pride of place at your table. This kind of cake requires time to create and your work should be admired and photographed before being devoured.

Birdcage Cake

2 x 15-cm/6-in. Classic
Victoria Sponge cakes
(see page 14) filled with
Buttercream (see page 20)
and raspberry jam

1 quantity Basic Buttercream
(see page 20)

sugar syrup (1 tablespoon
caster/granulated sugar
dissolved in 1 tablespoon
boiling water and allowed
to cool)

2 kg/4½ lbs white sugarpaste

250 g/1⅓ cups royal icing

gold metallic food paint

CMC powder

white Sugarpaste Roses (see
pages 78–79)

yellow buttercups (made using
a Buttercup cutter and
mould set)

15-cm/6-in. cake drum/circle
20-cm/8-in. cake drum/circle
icing turntable (optional)
serrated knife
marzipan spacers
parchment piping bag fitted with
a medium round piping
nozzle/tip
parchment piping bag fitted with
a small round piping
nozzle/tip
small paintbrush
gold ribbon

Serves up to 30

Birdcage cakes have become increasingly popular in recent years, most often seen atop pretty wedding cakes. I like to think of this as the perfect introduction to the world of cake carving; once mastered, it will unlock limitless cake crafting possibilities. If you wanted to add this cake to the top of a tiered cake, just remember to dowel the supporting tier as you would with any top tier (see pages 36–37).

1 Begin by filling your double-height cake with buttercream and jam on a 15-cm/6-in. cake drum/circle. I cannot stress enough how important it is to be sparing with your fillings in a cake like this as any excess filling will result in a lumpy finish, which we would like to avoid.

2 Refrigerate your naked cake for at 1–2 hours to allow it to firm up nicely.

3 You will be able to carve your cold cake using a large sharp knife. I prefer a serrated blade for this task. Carve only the very top portion of your cake to make it into a domed shape – angle your blade downwards from the centre of your cake and start to remove excess cake. You may find it easier to work with a turntable so that you can maintain the angle of your knife and simply rotate the cake. Once you are happy with the shape of your dome, you can gently rub the dome of your cake with your hand to smooth out any rough edges.

4 Crumb coat your cake with buttercream (see pages 26–29) before returning it to the fridge for 30 minutes.

5 Cover the 20-cm/8-in. cake drum/circle with 500 g/1 lb. 2 oz. sugarpaste by rolling out to the thickness of your marzipan spacers, brushing a little water on the drum and then laying the sugarpaste on top. Smooth your sugarpaste down using a straight-edge smoother and then trim the excess away as if you were trimming a pie dish. Smooth any rough edges by gently running your finger around the edge of the drum/circle. Finish the edges of your cake drum/circle with gold ribbon, secured with double-sided tape. Leave this to dry overnight.

6 Brush your cake with a scant amount of sugar syrup before covering in sugarpaste (see pages 32–35). The syrup will create the sticky surface that the sugarpaste needs to adhere to the cake. You should not find covering this shape to be any more taxing than covering a standard cake, but you will need to be aware of the extra height that you are working with. Work swiftly and always remember to smooth your paste upwards and never pull downwards on it, avoiding the potential of ripping. Leave your covered cake to dry overnight before decorating.

7 Fix your birdcage cake in the centre of your covered 20-cm/8-in. cake drum/circle with a little royal icing.

8 Roll a 5-cm/2-in. ball of sugarpaste and slice in half with a sharp knife. Affix one half of this ball to the top of your birdcage cake with a little water, reshaping with your fingers as necessary. Roll a smaller ball of sugarpaste and press down until flattened into a 2.5-cm/1-in. circle. Fix this circle of paste to the top of your paste dome with a dab of water.

9 To create a ring at the top of your cage, add a ¼ teaspoon of CMC to 50 g/1¾ oz. of sugarpaste and roll it into a sausage, twisting into a ring shape and allowing to dry overnight. This can then be fixed to the top of your cake with royal icing.

10 Roll a thin sausage of sugarpaste to a length of approximately 15 cm/6 in. and fix this around the bottom of your sugarpaste dome, trimming as necessary.

11 Fill a parchment piping bag fitted with a medium round piping nozzle/tip with royal icing and pipe a horizontal line of dots around the cage at the bottom point of the main dome and then repeat with a second horizontal line of dots roughly 2.5 cm/1 in. lower than this.

12 Fill a parchment piping bag fitted with a small round piping nozzle/tip with royal icing and use this to pipe vertical lines from top of your dome to the top line of dots and then from the bottom line of dots to the bottom of your cake.

13 Use your small piping nozzle to pipe a swirling pattern within the inch gap between your two lines of dots. Finish the very top of your cake dome with a ring of small dots piped around the sausage at the bottom of your sugarpaste dome. Finish the bottom of your birdcage cake with another line of dots, piped using your medium piping nozzle/tip.

14 Allow everything to dry for at least 2 hours before handpainting all of the decorative flourishes with gold metallic food paint. It takes a steady hand to paint those vertical lines so take your time. Decorate your birdcage with a few sugarpaste roses and buttercups, fixed to your cake with a little royal icing.

Floral Explosion Cupcakes

12 cupcakes in the flavour of your choice (see pages 14–18) baked in black foil cases

500 g/1 lb. sugarpaste

36 Sugarpaste Roses (see pages 78–79): 12 pale Dusky Pink, 12 Claret, 12 Hot Pink

96 green hydrangea blossoms (I've used Mint Green food paste colouring)

96 purple blossoms (I've used Royal Purple food paste colouring)

125 g/²⁄₃ cup royal icing

silver lustre spray

hydrangea cutter and mould
blossom cutter and mould

Makes 12

I always admired Alexander McQueen. There was one particular dress in his Spring/Summer 2007 show that really made an impact on me – it was a beautiful floor-length gown, festooned with stitched-in real flowers. This dress could only ever be worn once before they wilted and died. The transient nature of beauty means that it is here only fleetingly and, as such, should be thoroughly enjoyed. I like to think that if I wore a dress made of flowers, I would dance until every petal had fallen. Cakes, however pretty, are made to be eaten so this cupcake is one in the eye to anyone who ever tells you that a cake looks too pretty to eat, and a tribute to a great artist.

1 Prepare your cupcakes with a covering of white sugarpaste (see pages 30–31), concealing a cheeky mouthful of buttercream or cream cheese frosting.

2 The star of this show is your floral arrangement. All of your flowers can be made in advance and stored safely in a cardboard box for up to 1 week before you need to use them. Prepare Sugarpaste Roses (see pages 78–79), 12 in each shade of pink (pale Dusky pink, Claret and Hot Pink). You'll also need Mint-Green hydrangea blossoms and Royal Purple blossoms – around 96 of both of these. I know this sounds like a lot but they are ever so quick to stamp out. Leave them to dry when you're done.

3 Affix a bountiful arrangement of flowers to each cupcake with a tiny spreading of royal icing on the back of each one. Keep your smaller blossoms in little clumps and intersperse with roses.

4 Finish your cupcake with a spray of silver lustre to glaze your flowers. Delight as your guests wonder how they are to consume such a thing of beauty and then thank you when they eventually do!

Punk Rock Romance

20-cm/8-in. and 15-cm/6-in. Red Velvet Cake (see page 16) tiers, filled with Cream Cheese Frosting (see page 21)

1.5 kg/3¼ lbs white sugarpaste

125 g/²⁄₃ cup royal icing

silver metallic food paint

5 Wired Roses (see pages 72–73), coloured red

4 dowelling rods
parchment piping bag fitted with a medium round piping nozzle/tip
5-cm/2-in. thick tartan ribbon
15-mm/⁵⁄₈-in. thick black ribbon
plastic flower picks
gold 22-gauge floristry wire
small paintbrush

Serves up to 34

I consider it a rite of passage that every teenager should discover Punk Rock as if no one has ever heard it before. That energetic noise, with all of its rough edges, is the perfect balm to sooth the angst of adolescence. Used correctly, this same remedy can be relied upon as a lifelong outlet for any frustration associated with being a 'grown up'. The original scene of the 1970s has been romanticized, so here is a fittingly romantic nod to that scene.

1 Begin by preparing your Red Velvet Cake tiers filled with Cream Cheese Frosting and covering both in white sugarpaste (see pages 32–35). Dowel your 20-cm/8-in. tier and stack your 15-cm/6-in. tier on top (see pages 36–37).

2 Spoon 2–3 tablespoons of royal icing into a parchment piping bag (see pages 38–39), fitted with a medium round piping nozzle/tip. Use this to pipe a line of dots around the bottom of your top tier. Instead of dampening down the point left when you pull your piping nozzle/tip away, leave the points intact to create a ring of little studs. Allow these to dry for at least 1 hour before painting with silver metallic food paint.

3 Tie a tartan ribbon around the middle of your top tier. Leave the tails of your bow long enough so that they rest on the plate beneath your cake.

4 Trim the bottom of your cake with a simple black ribbon, secured at the back with a little royal icing.

5 Accessorize your cake with an asymmetrical arrangement of red Wired Roses. A small ball of leftover sugarpaste at the top of your cake will securely hold the stems of your roses and their leaves too.

6 My final nod to the aesthetic of Punk is a small heart of gold barbed wire made from gold floristry wire. To make barbed wire, first twist 2 full lengths of wire to create one spiralling double wire. Smaller single 5-cm/2-in. lengths of wire can then be twisted around the main wire twice each at regular intervals. Trim these smaller wires, leaving tiny points at either end to make the little barbs. Twist your finished length of barbed wire into a circle, pulling the bottom to a point and pressing the top into a heart shape, and sit it atop your top tier.

Carry on Glittered Heart Cookies

250 g/1⅓ cup royal icing

Red Extra paste food colouring

12 Basic Cookies (see page 19), cut using a 5-cm/2-in. heart-shaped cookie cutter

silver dragees

edible glitters in white, pink and red

3 parchment piping bags, each fitted with a small round nozzle/tip

3 squeezy plastic bottles

Makes 12

Inspired by the 'outfit' worn by Barbara Windsor in the classic British comedy film *Carry On Doctor*, these cookies bring a welcome sprinkling of sparkle to any tea-time indulgence. They are guaranteed to raise (at the very least) a smile when you divulge the identity of your muse.

1 Mix up your royal icing until it holds stiff peaks. Divide equally between 3 bowls, leaving 1 white and colouring the other 2 using your Red Extra paste food colouring. A scant amount of colour will result in pink icing, while a generous dollop creates scarlet red.

2 Spoon 2 tablespoons of each icing into a parchment piping bag fitted with a small round nozzle/tip (see pages 58–59). Cover your bowls of icing with clingfilm/plastic wrap to prevent them from drying out.

3 Pipe a line of icing around the edge of one of your heart cookies. You may find it easier to pipe this line in 2 halves – one from the cleft to the bottom point on the right-hand side, then turning your cookie upside-down and piping from the bottom point to the cleft again. This technique of icing cookies is known as 'flooding' so you are, in effect, piping a 'floodgate' that will contain the icing neatly on top of your cookie. Once you have piped this line, gently press silver dragees all the way around your cookie, being careful not to break the line. Repeat this for each cookie, making 4 of each colour.

4 Add sufficient cold water to your remaining royal icing to change the consistency from stiff icing to 'seven-second' icing. You are aiming for a runny consistency whereby a spoon removed while stirring the icing will leave a ripple that disappears in the count of seven, leaving a perfectly flat surface. Pour this icing into 3 separate squeezy plastic bottles, one for each colour.

5 Squeeze your runny icing on top of a cookie, leaving a 5 mm/¼ in. gap from the dragee-studded edge so that your runny icing has space to settle into. Gently tease your runny icing to the floodgate line using a cocktail stick/toothpick.

6 While the icing is still wet, sprinkle with edible glitter in the same colour as your icing to make it really sparkle. Do not be tempted to use glitter in a contrasting colour as this always ends up looking like sparkly grit!

Versailles Cake

20-cm/8-in. Lemon Drizzle
   Cake (see page 15)
1 kg/3$\frac{1}{4}$ lbs sugarpaste,
   coloured cerise (I've used
   Claret food colouring paste)
250 g/1$\frac{1}{3}$ cups royal icing,
   coloured hot pink (I've used
   Claret food colouring paste)
125 g/$\frac{2}{3}$ cup royal icing,
   white
metallic gold food paint
3 Sugar Magnolias (see pages
   100–101)

damask cake side stencil
   (I have used one from
   Designer Stencils)
sticky tape
small palette knife
parchment piping bag fitted with
   a medium round piping
   nozzle/tip
small paintbrushes
gold ribbon

Serves up to 20

There are few places that I could see myself living outside of London. The Palace of Versailles is one of them. Though I cannot quite put my finger on it, there is just something about that place that appeals to me. This cake is inspired by Louis XIV Mars Salon, its cerise satin damask-hung walls dripping with gilt gold decorations. This room was begging to be honoured in icing.

1 Begin by preparing your Lemon Drizzle Cake with a filling of Lemon Curd and Cream Cheese Frosting (see page 21) before crumb-coating your cake (see pages 26–29).

2 Cover your cake with cerise sugarpaste (see pages 32–35) and allow to dry overnight, stored safely in a cardboard cake box, so that you will not damage the surface of the cake as you decorate it.

3 Mix up 250 g/1$\frac{1}{3}$ cups of royal icing so that it holds peaks and colour to a shade of hot pink using the same Claret food colouring that you used for your sugarpaste. Using the same shade ensures that your 2 colours will not clash at all.

4 Line your cake side stencil up against the side of your cake (see pages 40–41). I find that this is made easier by wrapping a length of spare ribbon around the bottom of my cake to set the height that I need the stencil to sit at, and I use a little sticky tape to stick either end of the stencil to the cake. This is all rather fiddly, so take your time.

5 Take a small amount (for argument's sake, a blob measuring around 2.5 cm/1 in.) of dark pink royal icing on a palette knife and gently press this on top of your stencil. This is important – you do not want to push the royal icing into the stencil or start spreading it onto the stencil as it will just go underneath the stencil and make a mess. Go slowly, working with a small amount each time until you have covered your stencil.

6 Clean off your palette knife and angle it against your stencil so that the blade runs straight down the entire length of the stencil. Pull your palette knife along the side of the stencil to remove the excess royal icing. You may need to make 2–3 to do the whole length of the stencil.

7 Once you are happy that the excess has been removed, gently pull your stencil away from the side of your cake. Hold both ends of the stencil and pull towards you to minimise any spreading of the icing beneath.

8 You will now be able to see if there are any smudges in your design. If there are any mistakes, these can be cleared up using a damp paintbrush.

9 Allow your stencilled design to dry for 10 minutes before lining up your stencil once more to continue the pattern and repeating steps 5 to 8.

10 If your stencil does not repeat perfectly, and you end up with an area that is shorter than the stencil, you can get a little creative with the design at the back of your cake. If you use the sections at either end of your stencil to complete the larger sections of your damask pattern, the slight anomaly in the repeat will be barely noticeable.

11 Using a parchment piping bag fitted with a medium round piping nozzle/tip and filled with white royal icing, pipe a line of dots along the top edge of your damask design (see pages 38–39). Allow these dots to dry for 3 hours before painting with gold metallic food paint.

12 Set a small ball of left over cerise sugarpaste in the centre of your cake and crown your royally excessive masterpiece with blooms of Magnolia and foliage, their stems pushed into the ball of paste (see pages 100–101) to secure them. I have also created some Magnolia buds by wiring 3 of the smallest Magnolia petals together to create closed heads. Finish your cake by adding a gold ribbon around the bottom, secured at the back with a little royal icing. This cake is easily worthy of the most glamorous of tables, so celebrate in style with this one!

Rhapsody in Blue

20-cm/8-in. and 15-cm/6-in. Classic Victoria Sponge Cake tiers (see page 14)

2 kg/4½ lbs sugarpaste, coloured using Navy food colouring paste

250 g/1⅓ cups royal icing

pearlescent white metallic food paint

3 sugar Wired Roses in white (see pages 72–73)

2–3 sprigs of Sugar Bluebells (see pages 66–67)

25-cm/10-in. cake drum/circle
4 dowelling rods
white ribbon
baking parchment
scribe tool or cocktail stick/toothpick
sticky tape
parchment piping bag fitted with a small round nozzle/tip

Serves up to 34

There is something so intrinsically English about this shade of blue. The pattern that I have used to create the pearl motif around the sides of this cake is based upon one of the many pearl chokers in my jewellery box.

1 Prepare your Classic Victoria Sponge Cake tiers by filling them with raspberry jam and Buttercream, before crumb-coating them (see pages 26–29), and covering in blue sugarpaste (see pages 32–35). I have used Navy paste food colouring to get this lovely shade.

2 Cover a 25-cm/10 -in. cake drum/circle with leftover blue sugarpaste and fix your 20 -cm/8-in. tier in the centre of this drum. Dowel your 20-cm/8-in. tier (see pages 36–37) and trim your cake drum/circle with a white ribbon.

3 Trim a length of baking parchment to fit neatly around your 20-cm/8-in. tier (with no overlap) and a second length to fit around your 15-cm/6-in. tier. You will need approximately 66 x 10-cm/26 x 4 -in. for your 20-cm/8-in. tier and 48 x 10-cm/19 x 4-in. for your 15-cm/6-in. tier.

4 Fold the baking parchment collar for your 20-cm/8-in. tier into 6 equal sections and fold the collar for your 15-cm/6-in. tier into 4 equal sections. On both folded collars draw your pearl design in pencil. I have used a series of circles with every other one featuring a teardrop-shaped pendant at the end of 1, 2 or 3 vertical beads, arranged in a sequence.

5 With your folded collar rested on a tea/dish towel or other soft surface, use a scribe tool or a cocktail stick/toothpick to poke through the centre point of each pearl in your pattern. When you open up your collar, the pattern should repeat in tiny pin pricks. You will need to do this for both collars.

6 Wrap your collars around your cake tiers, securing with a little sticky tape, and use your scribe tool or cocktail stick/toothpick to poke through a mark for each pin prick to your cake. When you remove the collars you should see a clear pattern for piping your pearls.

7 Fill a parchment piping bag (see pages 38–39), fitted with a small round piping nozzle/tip, with royal icing and pipe tiny dots in the place of your pin pricked marks. Create your teardrop by dragging your piping nozzle/tip upwards instead of pulling directly away when you are happy with the size of the dot your have piped. Any peaks in your icing dots can be flattened down with a very lightly damp paintbrush as you go. Allow your piped pearls to dry for at least 1 hour before carefully painting with pearlescent white metallic food paint to bring them to life.

8 Carefully stack your 15-cm/6-in. tier on top of your 20-cm/8-in. tier. Top your cake with an arrangement of 3 white Wired Roses and Bluebells. Place a golf-ball sized ball of left over white sugarpaste at the middle of your cake and use this to push your flower wires into to hold your arrangement securely.

Baroquies

12 chocolate Basic Cookies, (see page 19), cut using a 5-cm/2-in. round cookie cutter

250 g/1⅓ cups royal icing, made with 1 teaspoon peppermint extract added

Mint Green paste food colouring (or similar shade)

gold dragees

parchment piping bag fitted with a small round nozzle/tip
squeezy plastic bottle
plastic piping bag fitted with a small round nozzle/tip
cocktail stick/toothpick

Makes 12

Could these be the most decadently divine minty cookies ever? Those swirling lines and the sparkle of gold are certain to impress. Stand one of these beauties next to the next cup of tea you serve up to an honoured guest and let me know how they go down.

1 Mix up your royal icing until it holds stiff peaks. Add Mint Green (or similar shade) paste food colouring until you have a pale shade of green.

2 Spoon 2–3 tablespoons of stiff, pale green icing into a parchment piping bag fitted with a small round nozzle/tip (see pages 38–39). Ensure that any icing you are not using is covered with clingfilm/plastic wrap to prevent it from drying out.

3 Pipe a line of icing around the top edge of a cookie. Once you have piped this line, gently press gold dragees all the way around your cookie, being careful not to break the line. You will find this easier if you work on half a cookie at a time, because the icing dries very quickly. Repeat this for each cookie.

4 Add sufficient cold water to your remaining royal icing to change the consistency from stiff icing to 'seven second' icing. You are aiming for a runny consistency where a spoon removed while stirring the icing will leave a ripple that disappears in the count of seven, leaving a perfectly flat surface. Pour all but 2–3 tablespoons of this icing into a squeezy plastic bottle.

5 Add more Mint Green paste food colouring to your remaining 'seven-second' icing to create a deeper shade. Spoon this icing into a plastic piping bag fitted with a small round nozzle/tip. This icing is very runny so I recommend that you insert a cocktail stick/toothpick into the piping nozzle before you fill the piping bag and use this again to plug the nozzle/tip any time that you are not using it.

6 Squeeze your pale green runny icing on top of a cookie, filling up the top but leaving a 5-mm/¼-in. gap from the dragee-studded edge so that your runny icing has space to settle into. Gently tease your runny icing to the floodgate line using a cocktail stick/toothpick.

7 While this icing is still wet, use your darker green icing to create a pattern of filigree swirls. You will need to work with one cookie at a time as the darker green icing should settle perfectly into the pale green icing and create a perfectly flat, smooth icing.

Famous & Fabulous

Judy Garland: Dorothy's Ruby Red Slippers

20-cm/8-in. Chocolate Mud Cake filled with Chocolate Buttercream (see page 20) and raspberry jam and covered with Chocolate Buttercream (see page 25–29)

raspberry jam

750/1⅔ lbs dark chocolate cigarillos

a little royal icing

fresh raspberries

red edible glitter

25-cm/10-in. cake drum/board
blue and white gingham ribbon (5-cm/2-in. and 15-mm/⅝-in. widths)

Serves up to 20

As a tribute to Judy Garland's most iconic film role, I first designed this cake for the wedding of a couple who did not want their cake to look too 'wedding-y'. They did, however, want to bring elements of retro glamour into their day, with plenty of sparkle, and were huge fans of Chocolate cake!

1 Set your Chocolate Mud Cake on a 25-cm/10-in. cake drum/board. Fill your cake with Chocolate Buttercream and raspberry jam, the very best you can afford.

2 Following the instructions on pages 25–29 (although you'll be using your Chocolate Buttercream instead of the basic one), cover the top and sides of your cake with Chocolate Buttercream and spread a little more around the exposed silver top edge of your cake drum/board. Professional cake designers always cover their cake drums/boards so this extra effort will result in a fabulous looking end product! Run a knife around the edge of your cake drum, as if you were trimming a pie dish, to tidy up the edges. Finish the edges of your cake drum with the 15-mm/⅝-in. thick blue gingham ribbon.

3 Gently press a continuous line of dark chocolate cigarillos onto the sides of your cake. Each cigarillo has a join line along it, where the chocolate has been rolled, and this should be the side of the cigarillo pressed into the cake. It just looks so much neater this way! Go slowly and ensure that your cigarillos are packed tightly together and are standing perfectly straight.

4 Tie your 5-cm/2-in. thick ribbon around the middle of your cake into a bow. To make the ribbon run neatly around a heart-shaped cake, you will need to stick the ribbon into the cleft of the heart with a small blob of royal icing. The trick is to first affix the middle point of your ribbon to the cake and wait for this to dry before carefully tying the bow. Failing this, there is no shame in the ribbon running across the cleft.

5 Fill the top of your cake with fresh raspberries. I think these look best when stood point up and packed into one single layer, though you are welcome to heap generous piles on top for a more rustic appearance. Brush your raspberries with a little raspberry jam, diluted with a teaspoon of boiled water, and sprinkle with red edible glitter to make them glisten and shine like Dorothy's ruby slippers.

Henri de Toulouse-Lautrec: La Belle Époque Cupcakes

12 cupcakes in the flavour of your choice (see pages 14–18) baked in gold foil cases

500 g/1 lb. sugarpaste, (I've used coloured pale green Mint Green paste food colouring)

250 g/1⅓ cups royal icing

gold dragees

gold edible sequins

parchment piping bag fitted with a medium round nozzle/tip
parchment piping bag fitted with a small round nozzle/tip

Makes 12

Inspired by the Art Nouveau movement in Paris at the turn of the 20th century, these little cakes are highly decorated and just a little decadent. The shades of green are inspired by the popularity of absinthe amongst the bohemian set that haunted the winding streets of Montmartre.

1 Cover your cupcakes with pale green sugarpaste (see pages 30–31).

2 Mix your royal icing to stiff peaks and colour to a darker shade of green using Mint Green paste food colouring.

3 Prepare 2 parchment piping bags, 1 with a medium round nozzle/tip, and the other with a small round nozzle/tip. Spoon 2–3 tablespoons of dark green royal icing into the first piping bag and 2–3 tablespoons of white royal icing into the second (see pages 38–41).

4 Use your medium round nozzle/tip to pipe a large dot into the centre of each cupcake. You are aiming for this dot to be around 1-cm/³/₈-in. diameter and perfectly round. Hold your piping bag so that the nozzle/tip points straight down onto your cupcake and squeeze gently until you are happy with the size.

5 Gently press gold dragees against the outer edges of this central dot so that it is surrounded by a rim of gold.

6 Pipe 8 smaller green dots (see page 161) in a circular pattern roughly halfway between the central dot and the edge of the cupcake.

7 Use your smaller piping nozzle/tip to pipe a fine line that will surround and encompass your 8 outer dragees. You can follow the pattern that I have used or simply pipe around the outer edge of each of these dragees. I have created 2 separate lines to incorporate every other dragee. This slightly asymmetrical symmetry is something I admire about the Art Nouveau movement.

8 While this fine line of icing is still wet, gently press gold edible sequins into it. You should have created a stunning Jade brooch motif that is certain to impress.

Audrey Hepburn: Breakfast at Tiffany's

20-cm/8-in. Red Velvet Cake (see page 16) filled and crumb-coated (see pages 26–29) with Cream Cheese Frosting (see page 21)

1 kg/2¼ lbs sugarpaste, coloured using Aqua paste food colour

100 g/3½ oz. white sugarpaste with ½ teaspoon CMC powder kneaded in

250 g/1⅓ cups royal icing

pearlescent white metallic food paint

light silver metallic food paint

500 g/16 oz. sugarpaste

silver and pearl dragees

66 x 10-cm/26 x 4-in. baking parchment collar, but trimmed to fit your cake perfectly
scribe tool or cocktail stick/toothpick
teardrop jewel silicone mould
parchment piping bag fitted with a medium round piping nozzle/tip

Serves up to 20

En homage to the iconic movie, I've adorned this cake with swags of piped pearls, a teardop-shaped brooch and an eye-catching white bow. All you need is a little black dress and you're good to go.

1 Begin by preparing your Red Velvet Cake with a filling and crumb-coat of Cream Cheese Frosting. Trust me, this is the only way to go with this cake!

2 Cover your cake with a smooth layer of the coloured sugarpaste (see pages 32–35). The exact strength of colour for a Tiffany blue is tricky to achieve but you can be more generous with the colour than you think. Allow your covered cake to dry overnight before decorating to avoid damage.

3 Wrap a length of baking parchment around the sides of your cake and trim to fit. Fold this collar into 4 equal sections and draw a semi-circle onto the top edge of your folded parchment — you may find it easiest to draw around a cup or a glass for this. Aim to make this semi-circle approximately 2.5 cm/1 in. from the top of your paper at its lowest point. Cut along the line that you have drawn and open up your parchment to reveal four equal swags. Wrap the collar around your cake, securing with a little tape, and carefully score along the swag lines with a scribe tool or cocktail stick/toothpick.

4 Make 4 teardrop-shaped jewels, pressing each one from a silicone mould using white sugarpaste mixed with CMC powder. You can make these in advance if you like and allow them to dry before attaching one to the bottom of each of your 4 swag lines with a little royal icing. If you cannot find a good teardrop jewel mould, you can pipe a teardrop with royal icing by first squeezing to make a large dot and then gently pulling your nozzle upwards as you stop piping to create a point at the top edge.

5 Fill a parchment piping bag, fitted with a medium round piping nozzle/tip, with royal icing. Holding your piping bag very close but not touching the surface of your cake, pipe 1-cm/⅜-in. dots along the swag line up to the jewel and then carrying on along the line after the jewel.

6 Once you have completed a line of dots, repeat with another line of dots directly below and then another so that you have 5 lines. Allow your dots to dry for 3 hours before painting with pearlescent white metallic food paint to make them shine. Use this same paint to paint the outside edges of your teardrop, painting the middle of each one with a light silver metallic food paint.

7 Crown your cake with an oversized white fondant bow, made using the same technique that we used to top the Valentines Day cake on pages 56–57. Press a small silver dragee into the middle of your bow and surround this with a ring of pearl dragees.

Giacomo Casanova: Venetian Romance

12 cupcakes in your choice of flavour (see pages 14–18), covered in deep purple sugarpaste fondant (see page 30–31), coloured using Grape Violet paste food colour

250 g/1⅓ cups royal icing

metallic gold food paint

gold dragees

parchment piping bag fitted with a medium round piping nozzle/tip

Makes 12

Casanova; a lover so legendary that generations of lotharios have been referred to by his name. The design for this cupcake is based upon an elaborate gilded mask – the traditional Venetian accessory to partying and pleasure-seeking – from the Carnevale di Venezia.

1 Begin by covering your cupcakes with a layer of purple sugarpaste using the technique described on pages 30–31. I have achieved this colour using a good helping of Grape Violet paste food colouring.

2 Mix your royal icing until it holds stiff peaks that curl over slightly.

3 Spoon 3–4 tablespoons of your royal icing into a parchment piping bag fitted with a medium round piping nozzle/tip (see pages 38–39).

4 Pipe swirling lines of filigree pattern onto the top of your cupcake. Keep your lines large and fairly open as we will be filing in the gaps. Allow this icing to dry for 30 minutes before carefully painting with metallic gold food paint.

5 Fill any conspicuous bare spots with gold dragees to make your cupcake sparkle.

7 Finish your cupcake by piping a line of white dots around the edge of the icing. Leave to dry for 30 minutes before painting with gold metallic food paint.

8 Box up your cupcakes, slap on an ornate mask, and head out to the party!

Elizabeth Taylor & Richard Burton
Hollywood's Golden Couple

20-cm/8-in. and 15-cm/6-in.
Lemon Drizzle Cake (see
page 15) tiers, filled and
crumb-coated (see pages
25–29) with Lemon
Buttercream (see page 20)

Marshmallow Meringue
Frosting (see page 23)

Sugar Hyacinths (see pages
66–67)

flowerpaste, coloured yellow
using Egg Yellow food
colouring paste

20-cm/8-in. cake drum/circle
4 dowelling rods
24-cm/10-in. cake drum/circle
side scraper
icing turntable
large palette knife
yellow ribbon
JEM bow cutter (large)
flower pick

Serves up to 34

Their 12-year marriage, briefly broken by a 16-month divorce and a remarriage, endures as one of the most fascinating Hollywood love affairs of the 20th century. Described universally as a tempestuous relationship, the frisson between these two glamorous and gifted stars is apparent in every scene that they played together, both on and off the silver screen. When Elizabeth Taylor first married Richard Burton in 1964, her ensemble was beautifully in-keeping with the era. In a canary-yellow chiffon gown, her hair festooned with swirls of white hyacinths and lily of the valley, Liz looked the epitome of sixties cool. This cake is for her.

1 Begin by preparing your 2 Lemon Drizzle Cake tiers with a filling and thin crumb-coating of Lemon Buttercream (see pages 25–29). Dowel your bottom tier (see pages 36–37) so that the dowelling rods stick up around 5 mm/¼ in. from the top of the cake. Refrigerate both tiers while you make your Marshmallow Meringue Frosting.

2 For this design, you will need to fix your 20-cm/8-in. tier to a larger 24-cm/10-in. cake drum/circle. Your 20-cm/8-in. cake should already be set on an 20-cm/8-in. cake drum/circle so a cross of double-sided tape in the centre of your 20-cm/8-in. cake drum/circle should be sufficient to stick the 2 together.

3 You can simply buttercream this cake but I think that the Marshmallow Meringue turns it into something a little more special.

4 Spread a generous coating of frosting across the top and sides of your 20-cm/8-in. cake, removing any excess with a side scraper. Place your cake on a turntable and gently press the tip of your palette knife against the top edge of the side of your cake. Without moving the blade, slowly turn your turntable so that you create a line in the frosting. As you reach one full rotation, gently move your blade down to create a second line directly under your first. As you continue to move around the cake, bring the blade downwards in this same way until you reach the bottom. The cake should now have a wonderful textured detail.

5 Tidy up the top edges using your side scraper, pulling all top edges into the centre of the cake.

6 Repeat step 4 with your 15-cm/6-in. tier and carefully stack on top of the 20-cm/8-in. tier. You will need to spread some extra frosting around the bottom of your top tier to conceal any gap or damage.

7 Spread a little frosting over the exposed silver edge of your 24-cm/10-in. cake drum/circle and trim with a yellow ribbon.

8 Decorate your cake with two arrangements of white sugar hyacinths. The best way to arrange these on a frosted cake is to tape the stems of your flowers together with floristry tape, bending the stems as necessary to make the shape that you want, and then gently lay these in position, the frosting holding the display in place.

9 I have also added sugar bows to my arrangement, made using yellow flowerpaste and a large bow cutter (see pages 62–63). Placed on the edge of your two tiers, the illusion is that the flowers have been hand tied.

Scarlett O'Hara Southern Belle

20-cm/8-in. Classic Victoria
  Sponge Cake (see page 14)
  filled with Cream Cheese
  Frosting (see page 21) and
  raspberry jam

1 kg/2¼ lbs sugarpaste,
  coloured using a scant
  amount of Honey Gold
  paste food colour

dark green dust colour

clear alcohol (optional)

white dust colour

250 g/1⅓ cups royal icing,
  coloured using a scant
  amount of Honey Gold
  paste food colour

Sugar Magnolia in white with
  foliage (see pages 72–73)

emerald green ribbon
small paintbrush
parchment piping bag fitted with
  a large leaf piping nozzle/tip

Serves up to 20

Well, fiddle-dee-dee, a cake inspired by Scarlett O'Hara? This one is sure to be the belle of the ball. *Gone with the Wind*, in all its Technicolor glory, is a feast for the eyes, and I hope that this cake is a feast for all of the senses! The design was inspired by the carefree beginnings of Scarlett's journey and the green dress that she wears to the barbeque at Twelve Oaks.

1 Prepare your Classic Victoria Sponge Cake, filling it with Cream Cheese Frosting and raspberry jam and cover with ivory coloured sugarpaste (see pages 32–35). A very tiny amount of any dark yellow tone paste colour (I have used a Honey Gold) will warm bright white sugarpaste into an ivory shade. Allow your icing to dry overnight before decorating to avoid damage.

2 Trim the bottom of your cake with an emerald green ribbon, securing at the back with a little royal icing.

3 Add a few drops of any clear alcohol to dark green dust colour to make an edible paint. You can use water if you would prefer not to work with alcohol but you will find that alcohol dries much faster. Prepare a second lighter shade of green paint using white dust colour and a small amount of dark green.

4 Use a small paintbrush to paint a floral pattern around the sides of your cake. I have taken my inspiration from the pattern of Scarlett O'Hara's green dress, featuring three open blooms, some foliage and some bell flowers. I began first with my pale green flowers, before adding the darker green details and finishing with white centres in my larger flowers. If this pattern is a little fussy to copy, you could always paint small ditsy blossoms in different shades of green. Repeat this pattern until the sides of your cake are covered.

5 Fill a parchment piping bag, fitted with a large leaf nozzle/tip (see pages 38–39), with 2–3 tablespoons royal icing and pipe a ruffle trim around the top edge of your cake. Angle your piping bag so that the opening of the leaf nozzle is horizontal and squeeze gently until the icing makes contact with the cake. Rock the piping nozzle back and forth, continuing to squeeze gently as you move around the top edge of your cake. The continuous line of icing should fold over itself, creating the illusion of ruffles.

6 Top your cake with a single white sugar magnolia and sit back as this cake garners all of the attention at your barbeque!

Beauty & The Beast: A Single Red Rose

1 Wired Rose, assembled with 2 lengths of 18-gauge wire (see pages 72–73)

green flower paste

green and brown dust colours

edible glue

20-cm/8-in. Chocolate Mud Cake (see page 17) filled with Chocolate Buttercream (see page 20) and covered with Dark Chocolate Ganache (see page 22) and Milk Chocolate Ganache (see page 22, but use 100 ml/3⅓ fl. oz milk chocolate and 50 ml/1⅔ fl. oz whipping cream)

1 dowelling rod
green floristry tape
green tissue paper
rose leaf plunger cutter (see pages 52–53)
ball tool
cocktail stick/toothpick

Serves up to 20

The Beast was cursed to remain in his terrifying form unless he could learn to love before the last petal fell from an enchanted rose. This single red rose will not shed any more of its petals but will float above your cake until it is devoured by a beauty. This cake is my homage to the films of Walt Disney and this one is my personal favourite.

1 Make your Wired Rose in advance using the technique described on pages 72–73. To enable your rose to stand upright, you'll need to insert 2 lengths of 18-gauge floristry wire through the middle of your cel bud and pull them down to form the stem of the rose. These are thicker wires than we would normally use for this task so you may find them tricky to manipulate. Build your rose with a maximum of 4 layers around the central bud so that it is not too heavy. Finish your rose with a calyx as usual.

2 Use your 5-petal cutter (again, see pages 72–73) to cut an extra 5 rose petals, separated using a small knife, and with their edges frilled all the way around using your ball tool. Leave these petals to dry on an uneven surface (crumpled up baking parchment works just fine).

3 Trim a wooden dowel to around 20-cm/8-in. long. Mark a height of 10 cm/4 in. on the dowel with a pencil to give you some idea of where the dowel will emerge from the top of your cake and tape the wires of your rose to the dowel with floristry tape. Try to balance your wires so that they surround the dowel, rather than just taping them to one side.

4 To thicken the stem of your rose, wrap a little tissue paper around the wires and continue to bind the stem in green floristry tape.

5 I have included 2 rose leaves taped to the stem. To do this, roll out the green flower paste to 2-mm/$\frac{1}{16}$-in. thickness and cut 4 identical rose leaf shapes using the plunger cutter (see pages 52–53). Paint one of your leaves with a little edible glue and a lay a length of green wire along the middle of the shape. Gently press your second leaf shape on top to sandwich the wire inside. Gently frill the edges of your leaf using a ball tool. You will need to replace your plunger cutter over your leaf and recut the sharp edges whilst also pressing the plunger to indent the veined details on the leaf. Repeat the process to create the second leaf. Allow the leaves to dry with movement before brushing with green dust colour on the surface of the leaf and brown dust colour around the edges. Thorns can be created by folding tiny lengths of tape into triangles as you bind the stem.

6 Gently tilt the head of your rose downwards. Try to maintain the centre of gravity by not bending the head too far away from the stem as the weight could pull the rose over.

7 Prepare your Chocolate Mud Cake by filling and crumb-coating it with Chocolate Buttercream, (see pages 25–28) and refrigerating it for 30 minutes. Because we will be covering the cake in dark chocolate, it is fine to crumb coat with Chocolate Buttercream.

8 Cover your cooled Chocolate Mud Cake with a generous spreading of Dark Chocolate Ganache. Straighten the sides and top edges of your cake as normal. Repeat this process by adding the milk chocolate ganache in patches over the dark chocolate ganache. This will be much thinner than your dark chocolate and should create a kind of glaze layer when spread around the sides and top with a side scraper. Fix a gold ribbon around the bottom of your cake, securing with a tiny dot of ganache.

9 Allow your ganache to set for 10 minutes before inserting the dowel of your rose straight down into the centre of the cake. Do this decisively as any wiggling may result in the dowel not holding securely.

10 Scatter your 5 red rose petals around the base of your rose and on the plate beneath your cake. I think this cake would be a wonderfully romantic centrepiece for any celebration of true love and I hope that you all live happily ever after.

Jay Gatsby: Deco Decadence

2 teaspoons CMC powder

500 g/1 lb. 2 oz. black sugarpaste (pre-coloured)

gold metallic food paint

20-cm/8-in. Lemon Drizzle Cake (see page 15) filled with Lemon Buttercream (see page 20) and covered with 1 kg/2¼ lbs white sugarpaste (see pages 32–35)

500 g/1 lb. 2 oz. sugarpaste

125 g/²⁄₃ cup royal icing

8 gold dragees

4 Wired Roses, 3 in gold and 1 in black (see pages 72–73)

24-cm/10-in. cake drum/circle
black ribbon
gold ribbon
gold lustre spray

Serves up to 20

This gold and black creation was inspired by the simple symmetry and straight lines of the Art Deco movement and the glorious decadence (not all of it legal, as Mr Gatsby knew only too well) that characterized the 'Roaring Twenties'.

1 Begin by creating your art deco inspired panels. These should be prepared at least 1 day in advance of when you want to affix them to your cake but can be made up to a week ahead of time, if stored safely in a cardboard box. I have made 8 panels, each measuring 8 cm/3 in. at their widest point and 8 cm/3 in. high – this is easy to remember, as it is always 8! You can use any design you like with these measurements or trace the one that I have used onto a little thin card to make a template.

2 Knead the CMC powder into the black sugarpaste (you seriously need to buy this pre-coloured as there is no amount of colour that you can knead into white sugarpaste to make anything other than a sticky mess) and roll out to 3 mm/⅛ in. thickness. Use your template to cut out 8 panels and leave these to dry overnight on a flat surface. Once your black panels have dried, use gold metallic food paint to paint lines to add detail to the shape. Follow the geometric lines of your panel.

3 Fill your Lemon Drizzle cake with a Lemon Buttercream or a Cream Cheese Frosting with a cheeky dollop of lemon curd mixed in, before covering in white sugarpaste. Cover a 24-cm/10-in. cake drum/circle with white sugarpaste and trim this drum/circle with a black ribbon secured at the back with a little royal icing. Once both your cake and covered cake drum/circle have dried for a few hours, attach your cake to the centre of your drum with royal icing. Wrap a gold ribbon around the bottom of the cake.

4 Stick your dried black and gold panels to your cake at evenly spaced intervals. The best way is to add one panel, just at the top of your gold ribbon, before adding the next directly opposite. Repeat this after turning your cake by a quarter turn. Now add your remaining panels, one each spaced perfectly between the panels you have already added. Do not be tempted to use too much royal icing to stick your panels on, as they only need a small amount and may slide off if you overload them.

5 Stud a single gold dragee into your sugarpaste-covered cake drum/circle at the middle point between each black sugarpaste panel. Spray 4 white Wired Roses with gold lustre spray to make them shine. The lustre will not completely cover each petal but will give a wonderful 3D effect, where the outer edges of your petals are very gold and the inner parts remain white. Spray from a distance to avoid beads of lustre building up on your petals. Leave these to dry for 10 minutes.

6 Place a ball of leftover sugarpaste in the centre of your cake and push the stems of your gold rose in so that they create a ring. Finish the cake with a single black rose pushed down into the middle of the golden roses, like an outsider in the midst of a world of gilt and glamour.

Marilyn Monroe Runnin' Wild

20-cm/8-in. Salted Caramel Cake (see page 18), filled and crumb-coated (see pages 26–29) with Salted Caramel Buttercream (see page 20)

White Chocolate Ganache (see page 22)

gold and silver dragees

gold and silver edible sequins

24-cm/10-in. cake drum/circle
scribe tool or cocktail stick/toothpick
silver ribbon

Serves up to 20

Marilyn Monroe is something of an idol of mine. Her performance as Sugar Kane in *Some Like it Hot* was undoubtedly her greatest, working under the genius of Billy Wilder, who knew just how to send up the screen image of his leading lady for comedic effect. Perhaps the best example of this synergy of star power and direction with a nod and a wink comes as Sugar performs 'I Wanna Be Loved by You' in a rather risqué gown. Marilyn is completely covered but the spotlight, finishing just above her bosom, makes her look naked save for a few sparkles. This sparkling cake is deceptively easy to make and contains just that extra hint of Sugar to make it all the sweeter.

1 Prepare your Salted Caramel cake with a filling and a thin crumb-coat of Salted Caramel Buttercream. Refrigerate to firm up a little while you get on with your White Chocolate Ganache. I recommend setting this cake directly onto a 24-cm/10-in. cake drum/circle to allow extra space for sparkle later on.

2 Mix up a quantity of White Chocolate Ganache and allow to cool until its consistency will permit easy spreading of a generous layer around the sides and over the top of your cake. Spread a thin layer of ganache over the silver of your cake drum/circle too.

3 Use your scribe tool or a cocktail stick/toothpick to mark 8 equal portions around the top edge of your cake – the easiest way to do this by eye is to mark the opposite points and then turn your cake a quarter turn to mark the opposite points again, finishing by making a mark in-between each of your marks.

4 Create a faint swag line to connect each of your points. This is intended only as a guide for our edible bling so does not need to be very precise, just try to keep the dip of each swag equal at around 2.5 cm/1 in. Use your gold and silver dragees to create a continuous series of short vertical lines, hanging down from below your swag line. These pieces should happily adhere themselves to the soft ganache with a gentle push.

5 Scatter gold and silver edible sequins over the top of your cake so that they fall onto the drum beneath. Trim the cake drum/circle with a silver ribbon to finish it beautifully.

6 Enjoy this sweet delight, which I sincerely hope is just about as far from the 'fuzzy end of the lollipop' as you can get.

Marie Antoinette: Rococo to Revolution

20-cm/8-in. and 15-cm/6-in.
Chocolate Mud Cake (see
page 17) tiers filled with
Chocolate Buttercream (see
page 20) and crumb-coated
(see pages 26–29) in
Vanilla Buttercream

1 kg/2¼ lbs sugarpaste,
coloured using turquoise
food paste colouring

1 kg/2¼ lbs sugarpaste

250 g/1⅓ cups royal icing

pearlescent white food paint

1 large and 1 small Wired
Rose, coloured pale pink
using dusky pink food paste
colour (see pages 72–73)
and 5 small Wired Roses,
coloured dark pink

pale blue Hydrangea Blossoms
(see pages 66–67)

pearl dragees

8 sugar rose leaves (see pages
52–53), cut using a rose
leaf cutter

24-cm/10-in. cake drum/circle
turquoise ribbon
4 dowelling rods
damask cake side stencil
small paintbrush
parchment piping bag fitted with
a medium round piping
nozzle/tip
rose leaf cutter

Serves up to 34

Marie Antoinette may never have uttered those legendary words 'let them eat cake', so I will! Nothing is as good for the soul as a party, and a party just isn't a party without a cake. There is also very little that cannot be solved with a healthy dose of Chocolate Mud Cake. So you gorgeous lot, it felt appropriate to conclude our time together with this design, inspired by Marie Antoinette's bedchamber and Peers Salon at The Palace of Versailles.

'Let them eat cake.' – Charlotte White

1 Begin by preparing your Chocolate Mud Cakes with a filling of Chocolate Buttercream and a crumb-coat of Vanilla Buttercream. Cover the 20-cm/8-in. cake with pale turquoise sugarpaste, and the 15-cm/6-in. cake with white sugarpaste using the technique on pages 32–35. Allow to dry overnight, stored in cardboard cake boxes.

2 Cover your 24-cm/10-in. cake drum/circle with white sugarpaste and trim its edge with a turquoise ribbon.

3 Mix up the royal icing so that it holds stiff little peaks. Remember to cover the icing in clingfilm/plastic wrap or a lightly damp towel whenever you are not using it.

4 Fix your 20-cm/8-in. cake to the centre of you 24-cm/10-in. cake drum/circle with a little royal icing. Dowel your 20-cm/8-in. cake using 4 dowelling rods (see pages 36–37).

5 Line your cake side stencil up against the side of your 20-cm/8-in. cake. Wrap a length of spare ribbon around the bottom of the cake to set the height that you'd liked the stencil to sit at, and use a little sticky tape to stick either end of the stencil to the cake. Take your time as it can be a fiddly job.

6 Take a small blob of white royal icing on a palette knife and gently press this on top of your stencil (the one I used came from Designer Stencils). This is important – you do not want to push the royal icing into the stencil or start spreading it onto the stencil as it will just go underneath the stencil and make a mess. Go slowly, working with a small amount each time until you have covered your stencil.

7 Clean off your palette knife and angle it against your stencil so that the blade runs straight down the entire length of the stencil. Pull your palette knife along the side of the stencil to remove the excess royal icing. You may need to make 2–3 scrapes to do the whole length of the stencil.

8 Once you are happy that the excess has been removed, gently pull your stencil away from the side of your cake. Hold both ends of the stencil and pull towards you to minimize any spreading of the icing beneath.

9 You will now be able to see if there are any smudges in your design. If there are any mistakes, these can be cleared up using a damp paintbrush. The stencil that I have used for this pattern is one standalone pattern, wth no need to line up the stencil to repeat the pattern. In this instance, to continue working on the cake all you will need to do is rotate the cake so that you are working on an area directly opposite your first stencil, and repeat steps 5–9.

10 Allow your stencilled design to dry for 10 minutes before working on any area near it, as you may damage it.

11 Once you have finished this process on your 20-cm/8-in. tier, you will need to repeat steps 5–9 on your 15-cm/6-in. cake using the turquoise royal icing. I used the stencil to create 4 patterns on this tier. When you have allowed both cakes at least 1 hour to dry, stack them.

12 Using a parchment piping bag fitted with a large open star piping nozzle/tip filled with white royal icing, pipe a beaded border along the bottom edge of each of the 2 tiers (see pages 38–39). Allow this border to dry for 3 hours before painting with pearlescent white food paint.

13 Crown your cake with a large pink wired rose, secured with a ball of sugarpaste. Complete a stunning spray of flowers by flanking your large rose with 1 smaller light pink rose, 5 smaller dark pink roses, scattered clumps of pale blue hydrangea blossoms (with pearl dragee centres) and some rose leaves to make a stunning spray of flowers.

Sources & Suppliers UK

Squires Kitchen
The Grange, Hones Yard
Farnham
Surrey, GU9 8BB
Tel: 0845 61 71 813/01252 260 263
www.squires-shop.com
*Creating, manufacturing and selling
products for cake decorating and
sugarcraft for almost 30 years*

Blossom Sugar Art Ltd
Dalton House
60 Windsor Ave
London, SW19 2RR
www.BlossomSugarArt.com
Tel: 0203 600 0198
*Wide range of sugar craft tools
and moulds*

The Ribbon Shop
171 Kenton Road
Newcastle upon Tyne, NE3 4NR
Tel: 0191 597 2892
www.theribbonshop.co.uk
*Extensive range of decorative ribbons for
all your cake decorating needs*

LittlePod
Tel: 01395 232 022
www.littlepod.co.uk
*Importers and producers of high-quality
real vanilla and chocolate ingredients.
Speciality is natural Madagascan vanilla
paste in a tube.*

Culpitt
Jubilee Industrial Estate
Ashington
Northumberland, NE63 8UQ
Tel: 01670 814 545
www.culpitt.com
*Leading supplier and manufacturer
of cake decorating and sugarcraft
products*

Cake Craft World
7 Chatterton Road
Bromley
Kent, BR2 9QW
United Kingdom
Tel: 01732 463 573
www.cakecraftworld.co.uk
*Wide range of cake decorations,
equipment, tools, books and packaging*

Knightsbridge PME
Unit 23 Riverwalk Road
Enfield, EN3 7QN
Tel: 0203 234 0049
www.cakedecoration.co.uk
*Home of the world-renowned PME
range of sugarcraft tools*

Cake Craft & Decoration Magazine
Tel: 02476 738 846
www.cake-craft.com
*Leading monthly magazine for all
those interested in cake decoration
and sugarcraft*

CelCakes & CelCrafts
Springfield House
Gate Helmsley
York, YO41 1NF
Tel: 01759 371 447
www.celcrafts.com
Innovative cake decorating products

Blue Ribbons Sugarcraft Centre
29 Walton Road
East Molesey
Surrey, KT8 0DH
Tel: 0208 941 1591
www.blueribbons.co.uk
*Supplies a complete range of cake
decorating supplies, including tools,
icings, cutters, food colours, ribbons,
moulds and cake decorations*

The Cake Decorating Company
Unit 2b Triumph Road
Nottingham, NG7 2GA
Tel: 0115 969 9800
www.thecakedecoratingcompany.co.uk
*Innovative cake decorating, chocolate
making, sugar craft and baking
company*

The Chocolatier: Aneesh Popat
www.the-chocolatier.co.uk
Absolutely delicious truffles

Sources & Suppliers US

Wilton
7511 Lemont Road
Darien, IL 60561
Tel: (630)-985-6000
www.wilton.com
Huge range of cake decorating supplies

Global Sugar Art
Tel: (518)-561-3039
www.globalsugarart.com
A comprehensive selection of cake and confectionery decorating products

Sugarcraft: A Baker's Paradise
3665 Dixie Hwy
Hamilton, OH 45015
Tel: (513)-896-7089
www.sugarcraft.com
Over 30 years' experience in supplying decorations for cakes, cookies, pies and more

Beryl's Cake Decorating & Pastry Supplies
5520 Hempstead Way
Springfield, VA 22151
Tel: (703)-256-6951
www.beryls.com
Cake circles, food colouring pastes, chocolate moulds, stencils and ribbons

Fiesta Cake Supplies
5746 Johnson St.
Hollywood, FL 33021
Tel: (954)-616-1100
www.suppliesforcakes.com
Cake boards, dummies, cutters, stencils, silicon and resin moulds, edible decorations and piping bags

Designer Stencils
2503 Silverside Rd.
Wilmington, DE 19810
Tel: (800)-822-7836
www.designerstencils.com
Family owned and operated business with over 3,000 stencils

Cake Carousel
1002 N. Central Exp. Suite 501
Richardson, TX 75080
Tel: (972)-690-4628
www.cakecarousel.com
Classes range from the basics of cake, candy and cookie decorating to the intricacies of crafting fondant figures and hand-made sugar flowers

Cake Connection
1948 Lansing Ave.
Jackson, MI 49202
Tel: (517)-990-0880
www.cakeconnection.com
Cake and candy supply shop including edible images and gelatin art

American Cake Decorating Magazine
Tel: (877)-467-1759
www.americancakedecorating.com
Key resource to the cake decorating community since 1995

International Sugar Art Collection by Nicholas Lodge
6060 Dawson Blvd., Suite F
Norcross, GA 30093-1230
Tel: (800)-662-8925
www.nicholaslodge.com

Teaches all levels and aspects of sugar art, and cake decorating

Index

Icing Templates

You can photocopy or trace this page in order to practice the piping techniques for dots, lines and circles, as explained on page 39.

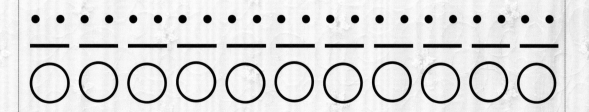

Acknowledgments

A nod, a wink and a hug to everyone who has aided the transition of this book from mad ideas to shelf – and kitchen! Special thanks to Nathan for working so hard on this project from start to finish. To Julia and Cindy for your encouragement and support. To Leslie for putting together an incredible creative team – my darling Tony whose creative vision brought mad ideas to life, my hero Dan who can not only create magic in a lens but make me laugh in the midst of the madness. To Maria for overseeing the creation of these images and for turning words into works of art. To Lauren and Jen, for believing in this book – I genuinely appreciate everything that you do.

To Anna-Louise at Fork Off Management for looking after me and always looking out for me. To Jez for putting up with my diva requests and to the gorgeous Sarah at Sarah's DooWop Dos for making me feel amazing in front of the camera. To Gerry at Glamour Bunny for providing the white wiggle dress that has become known as my 'chef's whites'.

To all of the fantastic suppliers who provided the means to create these designs; Natalie at Squires Kitchen, Ricky at Culpitt, Clara at The Ribbon Shop, Louisa at Blossom Sugar Art, Janet and the team at LittlePod.

To my wonderful family and urban family, I am short on space to name you all but rest assured you will all be thanked in person, with a glass or two raised in your honour, for your support.

To my darling Chris, with thanks for your constant love and kindness, this is for you.